HAUNTED HIKES

REAL LIFE STORIES OF PARANORMAL ACTIVITY IN THE WOODS

MAREN HORJUS

FALCON®

Guilford, Connecticut

An imprint of Globe Pequot
Falcon and FalconGuides are registered trademarks and Make Adventure Your Story is a trademark of Rowman & Littlefield.

Photos © istockphoto.com
Except photo 181 by Maren Horjus

Distributed by NATIONAL BOOK NETWORK

British Library Cataloguing in Publication Information available

Library of Congress Cataloging-in-Publication Data available

ISBN 978-1-4930-3064-4
ISBN 978-1-4930-3055-2 (e-book)

∞™ The paper used in this publication meets the minimum requirements of American National Standard for Information Sciences—Permanence of Paper for Printed Library Materials, ANSI/ NISO Z39.48-1992.

Printed in the United States of America

Contents

CONTENTS

CONTENTS

CONTENTS

CONTENTS

Introduction

FEAR IS a good thing, if only because it reminds us that we're human. Go for a walk in the woods if you've forgotten. Away from the din of calendar alerts, unread e-mails, and urgent notifications, the world shrinks to the size of one human being. And there, in that scale, is where your senses are awakened.

It's where a rustling in the underbrush can steal your breath, where a flicker of movement around the next switchback can send your heart thudding percussion in your eardrums. It's where your mind is freer to reconsider what you once thought to be true, and it's where I hope you are when you read—and later, recall—the stories in this book.

These stories are a mix between old and new, widely told and seldom heard, but they all share the same DNA: They center around our wild places.

This isn't to say that our cities and "frontcountry" are immune to ghost stories, but our natural lands—our old-growth forests, crinkle-cut mountains, redrock canyons, salt marshes, airy balds, and everything in between that characterizes America's wilderness—are shrouded in mystery. Or maybe it's just that there, where the world is untamed and unrestricted, we notice it.

Some of the stories on the following pages are purely objective recounts of legends ever-present in our history. Others are more speculative in nature, my personal spin based on my own research, interviews, and faculties. They span time, from our country's earliest beginnings, like the ancient tale of Princess Noccalula or the elusive Lost Paradise, to our more recent history, like the failed Letchworth Village asylum. Some explore the more paranormal, like the Bell Witch or the Hurricane Haint, while some examine crimes like the Shenandoah slayings and characters like Charles Manson whose violence, for all intents and purposes, has bled into the present. Still others are less scary than they are puzzling—who or what is responsible for the Carolina bays? Why have so many people perished on Rainier and Mt. Washington?

My hope in putting together this book was to explore these tales, the fabric of our wild places, with a journalist's eye and a child's wonder. But these stories aren't mine; they're ours, as hikers and people who believe in the supernatural power of wilderness, and I believe it's our duty to preserve them.

You can do your part in two ways. One, share these stories, preferably around a campfire in the untrammeled backcountry, but the setting doesn't matter. And two, let yourself get scared. The stories in this book should remind us that our peace is not guaranteed. The wilds around us don't owe us anything and are totally unpredictable.

So the next time you're on a lonely trail and you spy the faintest twinkle of movement or hear a whisper from somewhere in the underbrush, let your heart patter in your chest. Let it beat in your ears. Consider that maybe it's something more—or that it's the start of something that we should include in Volume Two.

Northeast

The Bennington Triangle

Glastenbury Mountain, Long Trail, Green Mountain National Forest, Vermont

I T'S IMPOSSIBLE to know what Paula Welden was thinking when she awoke on December 1, 1946. It was a Sunday. Perhaps she had penciled a hike into that small calendar square all along. Or maybe going for a walk in the woods was spontaneous—an afterthought when she finished her shift in the campus dining hall. Welden, a sophomore at Bennington College in Vermont at the time, liked the outdoors and painting. She was majoring in art, but reportedly losing interest in the subject, and supposedly dating someone long-distance, but hiding the news from her father. She was eighteen—and acting like it. So maybe it isn't necessarily odd that she returned to her dorm room and announced to her roommate that she was "taking a long walk." But it is strange that she never returned.

That afternoon, around 3 p.m., Welden left her dorm room wearing a fur-lined red parka and blue jeans and hitched a ride to the historic, 272-mile Long Trail. Famous as the country's first long-distance hiking path, the Long Trail runs the length of Vermont, undulating across the spine of the Green Mountains. One of its highlights comes in the form of 3,748-foot Glastenbury Mountain, a high point that sentinels over a sea of New England hardwoods in the southwest corner of the state. It's not an easy walk—more than 9 miles deep in the backcountry—but the trailhead is just a 10-minute ride from Bennington College and presumably where Welden was headed.

There are only a few reports of people she may have encountered, including the owner of a nearby gas station and the man who drove her up to VT 9. A couple of people reportedly saw her walking along the highway in the direction of the trailhead around 4 p.m.

When she didn't return from her walk, Welden's roommate allegedly alerted authorities, launching a campus-wide search. Community members fanned the area, while Welden's family offered a $5,000 reward to anyone who could locate their daughter. Newspapers hired private eyes. The fruitless search is said to have ultimately given rise to the Vermont State Police. Plainly, Paula Welden had vanished.

Oddly, though, Welden's disappearance was neither the first—nor the last—to occur in the area around Glastenbury Mountain. A year before, a hunting guide had gone missing and was never recovered. The area claimed another in 1949 and two more in 1950.

Despite thorough investigations at the time and subsequently, no one has ever discovered who or what is responsible for the disappearances. Some people believe there's a Bigfoot-like monster roaming the area,

while others have suggested the existence of sinkholes and interdimensional portals. Perhaps there was a serial killer, or maybe the mountain is just cursed. Since we can't ask Paula Welden, you'll have to see for yourself.

DO IT

Pick up the Appalachian/Long Trail from VT 9 (42.885110, -73.115580) and take it 9.4 miles north to the Glastenbury summit. Find established campsites near the mountaintop, or leave the tent at home and grab a spot in the Goddard Shelter (first-come, first-served) near mile 9.1. Retrace your steps the way you came for an 18.8-mile out-and-back, or arrange a shuttle car and thru-hike to Kelley Stand Road (43.061171, -72.967758) below Stratton Mountain, making it a 20.4-mile point-to-point hike.

The Weeping Woman

Bash Bish Falls, Bash Bish Falls Trail, Bash Bish Falls State Park, Massachusetts

BASH BISH. Bash bish. Bash bish.

Whisper it aloud and it may sound like water coursing off a schist precipice and plunging into a deep, aquamarine pool. Of course, if you're standing at the base of Bash Bish Falls's final, 80-foot drop and you hear it, it could be the water—or the distressed spirit of Bash Bish herself.

According to legend, Bash Bish was a beautiful, young Mohican woman. She was wise and honest and—when accused of committing adultery—innocent. She stood before the tribal elders in a council meeting and pled her innocence, but they didn't believe her. Instead, Bash Bish was sentenced to a cruel death. She would be tied to a canoe and released into the brook upstream of the waterfall that ultimately cascades some 200 feet to the basin below.

At the moment that she lurched over the outcropping, tumbling toward the rocky depths, Bash Bish, the story goes, looked out to her executors and beams of sunlight ringed her face. Colorful butterflies fluttered around her, seemingly shielding her. The elders watched the canoe plummet into the pool beneath the falls and later even recovered its remains—but no girl was ever found. The villagers concluded that Bash Bish must have been a witch.

But the story doesn't end there. Bash Bish left a daughter, a legitimate one, named White Swan. White Swan was clever and beautiful and fell in love with the tribal chief's son, Whirling Wind. But when White Swan was unable to provide children to her lover, depression seized her. Every day, she'd walk to the top of the falls to be alone and seek solace from her mother's spirit.

Whirling Wind, meanwhile, loved White Swan sincerely and would bring her gifts every day in an attempt to break her depression. One day, he followed her to the top of the cataract and opened his hands to offer her a butterfly that was as white as snow. White Swan, believing the gift to be a sign from her late mother, quickly sprung from her perch and dove head-long into the falls. The white butterfly followed her, fluttering in her wake. Whirling Wind leapt after his love, tumbling down the 80-foot drop. The villagers would recover Whirling Wind's pummeled body, but—as before—there would be no sign of White Swan.

Today, people can hike to the very spot Bash Bish and her daughter White Swan jumped. They can also walk to the pool where the women were never seen again. There, if you look closely, you can see the outline of a woman, thought to be Bash Bish, behind the falls. It's where she ushers other people to follow in her footsteps and jump into the pool, *bash bish, bash bish, bash bish.*

DO IT

For the best hike to Bash Bish Falls, begin at the South Taconic trailhead (42.116429, -73.506167) in Taconic State Park, New York. Take the South Taconic Trail about 0.8 mile east, crossing into Massachusetts's Bash Bish State Park. From there, take the Connector Trail roughly 0.7 mile to the Bash Bish Trail. The Bash Bish Trail circles 1 mile back to the South Taconic trailhead, passing viewpoints of the falls and a short spur to the base. Note: Swimming (voluntarily) is not allowed in Bash Bish Brook or the basin below Bash Bish Falls.

Behind Enemy Lines

Mt. Adams, King Ravine Trail, White Mountain National Forest, New Hampshire

I N MANY ways, Robert Rogers was ahead of his time. At the age of 22, the young man was already outwitting authorities, skillfully avoiding trial for counterfeiting. By 24, he had already developed and codified a set of twenty-eight basic rules for outsmarting ene-mies that the Army Rangers still use today. He had a kooky way of doing things, which maybe you'd expect from a counterfeiter, and his methods were extremely radical for the time, focusing more on intricate strategy than assault tactics ("If you have the good fortune to take any prisoners, keep them separate, till they are examined," rule number 5). So when the French and Indian War engulfed the colonies in the mid-1750s, it was Rogers, the kid from New Hampshire, who was suddenly responsi-ble for raising and commanding an infantry corps that would be charged with reconnaissance and special operations.

Though they didn't have the sort of prestigious training the Royal Crown provided, Rogers's ragtag team of New Englanders was inti-mately familiar with the terrain in the area. They had grown up among the wooded crowns of the Whites and the boulder-choked ravines of the Israel River valley and knew, almost instinctively, how to move through the territory. The team, dubbed Rogers's Rangers, saw great success in engagements from 1755 to 1758. And so, when word spread that there was a tribe of some 300 Abenaki up by the St. Francis River in present-day Canada who had tortured two British officers and raided communities as far south as Massachusetts, there was no doubt who would be appointed to take them out. It's impossible to say what Rogers did when tasked with the mission, but licking his chops would certainly have been in character.

However, the special operation didn't go as planned. After an accident involving gunpowder, Rogers's crew of 200 was almost instantaneously winnowed down to 140. As the dismantled company encroached on Missisquoi Bay at the northern end of Lake Champlain—where provisions awaited—Rogers sensed they would be ambushed and had to deliver the hard news to his men: They would not be restocking food and supplies. No, they would be veering into the swamplands to take a most circuitous (and wet) route to St. Francis, a route no one expected them to take. So Rogers and his loyal men did what they did best: changed course. They spent a week trudging 50 miles through boggy hardwood forests before the French gave up pursuit.

They barely slept, they barely ate, they barely drank, but Rogers's Rangers miraculously reached their destination at the banks of the St. Francis River on October 3, 1759, three weeks after their departure from Fort Crown Point in present-day New York.

First order of business, Rogers's Rangers sent out a team of scouts ("When locating an enemy party of undetermined strength, send out a small scouting party to watch them," rule number 28). And their namesake, of course, was not the sort of man to let another enjoy all the action, so he volunteered to lead. Dressed in Abenaki garb, Rogers and the scouts observed the Natives performing some sort of war dance—an indication that they themselves were preparing for a major raid or attack. Rogers needed to act fast.

The scouts fled back to their company and planned their assault: Rogers's Rangers would surround the village to attack from all angles, preventing any escapees. At 5 a.m. on October 4, mayhem ensued upon the sleeping village. Murder raged with no pity; Rogers's men mercilessly shot the Abenaki, stabbed them with bayonets, sliced their throats, smashed their skulls with tomahawks, and punctured every canoe they could find, effectively trapping the villagers inside the war zone. They set wigwams on fire and ransacked every structure they could find, including a small, Jesuit mission, from which they looted coins, a ruby ring, gold, and a 10-pound silver statue of the Virgin Mary carrying baby Jesus.

At this point, facts mix with legend and the reader is left to make his or her own assumption about who or what is responsible for what happened next. It's believed that a deep voice echoed through the conflagration of the mission, cursing Rogers's Rangers. *Hunger and death will follow you,* it proclaimed. The rangers, terrified, fled. Rogers broke his retreating army into smaller groups and instructed them to meet at a point along the Connecticut River some days later, where supplies would be waiting ("If the enemy is so superior that you are in danger of being surrounded by them, let the whole body disperse, and every one take a different road to the place of rendezvous appointed for that evening," rule 10).

But, as though ordained by the mysterious voice, the supplies weren't at the river. And most groups failed to show up, regardless. Some, it's believed, were pursued and killed by the French. At least one group suffered cannibalism from its own ranks. But, most notably, one of the missing crews was the group of men responsible for hauling the cursed gold from the mission.

The group of four men who were carrying the loot stumbled off-course when they encountered a freak, early-fall snowstorm. Catching their bearings, they opted to hightail it back to Concord, but they were so weak from sleep deprivation, hunger, and exposure, that they couldn't go on. They hid the treasures they'd pillaged somewhere among the braided creeks north of 5,794-foot Mt. Adams. And then, one by one, each of the four men perished.

DO IT

Hikers have reported seeing the ghosts of Rogers's Rangers, emaciated and crawling, in the valley north of Mt. Adams, but treasure is more exciting: While some of the gold and silver artifacts have been located in the area, no one, to this day, has found the silver Virgin Mary. Look for it on the King Ravine Trail, one of the country's most challenging day hikes, and a likely route of Rogers's Rangers. From the Appalachia trailhead on US 2 in Randolph (44.371526, -71.289310), link the Air Line and Short Line Trails about 3 miles to the King Ravine Trail, which reconnects with the Air Line Trail to spin-around views atop Adams. Note: You must be ranger-fit; the path gains nearly 4,500 feet of elevation in one 4.5-mile slog.

The Palatine Light

Sandy Point, Cow Cove, Block Island National Wildlife Refuge, Rhode Island

Into the teeth of death she sped
May God forgive the hands that fed
The false lights over the rocky head!

O men and brothers! What sights were there!
White up-turned faces, hands stretched in prayer!
Where waves had pity, could ye not spare?[1]

THE POOR *Princess Augusta* was doomed from the start. The ship set out from Rotterdam in 1738, carrying some 340 passengers seeking to escape the religious authority of the Palatinate. She was headed for Philadelphia, but almost immediately hit a strong tide and heavy swell. Neither abated, and before long *Augusta* was up against gale-force winds and, soon enough, a relentless blizzard. Some of the food onboard spoiled, and the drinking water contracted some sort of bacteria. *Augusta* lost a mast, her captain, half her crew, and more than half of her passengers to exposure, starvation, dehydration, and illness by the time she limped up to the East Coast.

On December 27 of that year, *Augusta*—later called the *Palatine* by the press—ran aground on Block Island, a small, 10-square-mile land mass off the coast of Rhode Island. Legend, however, has it that she was lured by false signal lights. Rhode Island had suffered an extremely harsh winter and the islanders were at their wits' end. They conspired to trick the acting captain to dock on Block Island and then they ravaged the

Augusta. According to the tale, they stole everything from supplies to the clothes off the passengers' backs, completely draining its stores. And then, with some passengers still trapped inside, they set it ablaze and pushed it out to sea.

If lighting fire to *Augusta* was supposed to hide their indiscretions, the islanders failed. Every December, people report seeing the ship, radiating amid a glow of flames, bobbing in the Block Island Sound.

But the year went round, and when once more
Along their foam-white curves of shore
They heard the line-storm rave and roar,

Behold! Again, with shimmer and shine,
Over the rocks and the seething brine,
The flaming wreck of the Palatine*!*

DO IT

First, take a ferry to Block Island (blockislandferry.com), then hitch a ride to the northern terminus of Corn Neck Road (41.224559, -71.567273). On foot, follow the beach northwest about a mile to Sandy Point, the northernmost tip of the island, where Princess Augusta supposedly ran aground. The Palatine Light is believed to return every year at some point between Christmas and New Year's; scan north and west for a bluish, luminous triangle that flickers in and out of sight. (If you have time, explore the Clay Head Preserve trail network on the northeastern point of the island; it's a mecca for migratory songbirds.)

The Lake Monster

Lake Champlain, Champlain Nature Trail, Button Bay State Park, Vermont

BIGFOOT MAY be the most well-known monster in North American lore, but he has company. You could argue that there are at least a dozen more inhuman denizens—including a few in this book—roaming our wild areas. Science, physical and paranormal, makes an interesting case for some, but they all tend to rely solely on witness accounts. Strip away the gorilla suit, and there's really only one American monster whose existence is supported by strong photographic evidence. That distinction belongs to none other than Champ, the serpentine monster of Lake Champlain.

Native Americans were, of course, the first to witness Champ, but the story didn't really gain traction until the lake's namesake, French explorer Samuel de Champlain, claimed to have seen Champ in 1609. He wrote in his log that he spied a lake monster with silvery scales, sharp teeth, and a snakelike body about 5 feet long and as thick as a man's thigh. Since then, some 300 individuals have reported seeing the creature.

That's all good and well, but you're probably not convinced. If you need harder evidence, consider Googling "Sandra Mansi." In July 1977, Mansi and her then-fiancé and two kids went for a scenic drive around Lake Champlain. The sliver-shaped lake stretches more than 130 miles north along the state line between New York and Vermont into Quebec, its sapphire-blue water pooling between the Adirondacks and Green Mountains. Mid-summer in Addison County brings temps in the 80s, so it's not hard to imagine the new family pulling over to splash and relax in a small cove overlooking the postcard-worthy scene. At some point, Mansi noticed a disturbance in the water. A reptilian creature with a humped back and long neck, like a brachiosaurus, breached the surface, sending ripples propagating out to the shoreline. While her fiancé shouted to the children to get out of the water, Mansi grabbed her Kodak Instamatic and snapped what would become the most famous photo of an American monster.

Still not convinced? Here's another one for you: Search YouTube for "Eric Olsen Champ." The year 2009 brought another layer to Champ's legacy when a quick-thinking tourist had the mind to capture almost two minutes' worth of cell phone video of a serpentine creature swimming to shore.

DO IT

You could spend a lifetime knocking out hikes in the area around Lake Champlain and never get bored, but if lake monster sightings are what you're after, head over to Button Bay. South of Burlington, the area is home to some of the most famous Champ sightings. Park in the state park (44.182184, -73.360802), and explore the patchwork of paths along the bay. Follow the shore west to the point of the peninsula and loop back to make a 1.5-mile circuit. Keep your eyes peeled for ripples.

The Headless Hitchhiker

Catherine Mountain, Catherine Mountain Trail, Hancock County, Maine

T AKE THE short, winding route to the top of Catherine Mountain in Down East Maine, and you'll score an eyeful: the deep-blue waters of Tunk Lake, the serpentine channels of Spring River Lake, the granite crags of Tunk Mountain, the surrounding slopes blanketed in fall-perfect foliage, and, maybe, a headless woman in a white dress.

Locals around here tell a story of Catherine, the 961-foot hill's namesake. Sometime in the 1920s, Catherine was a young employee at a lodge nearby. It was a swanky spot, one where wealthy flatlanders would stop by on vacations to the Down East, likely to escape Prohibition-era laws. Catherine, the legend goes, took a mid-shift break one day to go for a ride through Black's Woods with a male companion. She sat in the passenger seat of his Ford Model T as the two cruised through the corridor of birches and maples, past peekaboo vistas of misty mountains and mirror-like ponds. As the two hurtled around a bend, however, the man lost control of the car. The Model T careened off the road, plunging into the frigid depths of Fox Pond. Though the man's body was never recovered, Catherine's supposedly was—albeit, headless. She had been decapitated in the crash.

The legend continues: Catherine's ghost still wanders the stretch of ME 182 by Fox Pond looking for a ride. People have reported seeing her in a flowing white dress on the shoulder of the road. Some have described a transparent figure, others have claimed to see her opaque—but headless. She takes many forms, but the tale is clear: If you don't stop for her, regardless of her appearance, she will haunt you. Locals like to tell the story of a salesman who was traveling along ME 182 at night. He saw the headless ghost ambling along the road and didn't stop to pick her up (which seems fair), but when he looked in his rearview mirror, he saw her sitting in his backseat. He panicked (also fair), lost control of his car, and careened over the guardrail and into Fox Pond, suffering the same fate that Catherine herself had so many years before.

It's unclear what would happen if you spotted the ghost while hiking, rather than driving, but it seems appropriate to assume that climbing the mountain named after the ghost is at least a nice way to pay your respects. And no matter what you choose to believe, it should be noted that divers have made public record of there being a preserved Ford Model T at the bottom of Fox Pond.

DO IT

You can knock out the 1.5-mile out-and-back to Catherine's summit in a few hours. Find the trailhead off a road colloquially known as Dynamite Brook Road (off Black Woods Road, aka ME 182) near 44.618566, -68.103254. From there, take the blue-blazed Caribou Mountain Trail about 0.3 mile past mossy boulders and a fern-lined creek to a junction. Split north (hiker's left) onto the Catherine Mountain Trail and take it to the top where views await.

A Stitch in Time

Franconia Notch, Kinsman Ridge Trail, Franconia Notch State Park, New Hampshire

WHAT IF time disappeared? What if there was a spell you simply were not able to account for? For Barney and Betty Hill, it was as though they blinked and someone pulled the rug out from under them. Two hours were gone. The rest of the world moved through time, but the Hills stalled.

It was a balmy evening in the late summer of 1961, and the Hills, a middle-aged couple from Portsmouth, were driving home after vacationing in Montreal. There were quicker ways home, but the Hills chose to take US 3, a scenic road that runs the length of New Hampshire. Near Lancaster, Betty observed a bright light in the sky that oddly outshone the stars. She pointed it out to Barney and, unbelievably, the ball of light moved. It dipped beneath the moon, and Betty surmised that perhaps it was a truly incredible falling star. But then the light moved back above the moon. It swelled, as though it were either growing in size—or encroaching on the Hills' Chevy Bel Air.

The Hills pulled over at a campground near Twin Mountain so Barney could retrieve a small pistol from the trunk of the car—just in case. Betty picked up the couple's pair of binoculars and peered through the lenses toward the odd light, now flashing different colors and moving across the moon. "It's probably a commercial airliner heading to Montreal," Barney suggested. But, the thirty-nine-year-old man quickly switched tracks when the aircraft began descending rapidly. "This is not a plane."

The Hills clambered back in the car and drove frantically toward Franconia Notch, a famous mountain pass in the Whites. The couple observed the craft hover above Cannon Mountain, a rocky massif west of I-93. Betty scanned through the binoculars and was shocked to see the object was shaped like a saucer and appeared to be rotating. "Drive faster!" she commanded her husband, as the couple sped down I-93. And then Betty's heart sank. The aircraft began descending—rapidly—straight toward the car. Barney slammed the brakes and the couple watched, panicked, as the huge saucer hovered 80 feet above them. The craft was so close, Barney could see a group of figures with gray skin and bulbous, black orbs for eyes staring at him through the windows of the ship. They seemed to be looking right at him. Barney knew—though no one said a word—he was to stay still.

Fins telescoped out of the saucer amid blinking red lights, and a long structure, like a stairway, descended from the bottom to the ground. "They're going to capture us!" Barney shouted, as he revved the engine. He maneuvered the Bel Air south on I-93, the craft following in hot pursuit. The car vibrated and tingling sensations coursed through each of the Hills' bodies. High-pitched buzzing noises tore through the night air.

And then, nothing.

Two hours later and 35 miles farther south, the Hills came to. They recalled the terror of being chased, and then, suddenly, they were somewhere outside of Ashland, with no recollection of how they ended up there—or what had happened in the two previous hours.

The Hills were not outrageous people. They didn't have criminal records or any previous interest in the topic of UFOs. He was a humble postal worker and she a social worker. They knew their story would seem unbelievable, but they filed reports with the Air Force and the National Institute of Crime Prevention anyway. In addition to relaying the events of their encounter with the humanoids, they noted a few other oddities, like the series of shiny, concentric circles on the trunk of their Bel Air and that when they moved a standard compass near the spots, the needle spun erratically. Betty submitted her dress, which was ripped and blanketed in a weird pink powder, as evidence.

But nothing happened. Some officials suggested that they had mis-identified Jupiter, but the Hills knew better and, eventually, sought closure from a psychiatrist who specialized in hypnosis. It was a breakthrough: Through hypnosis, the Hills recovered the two lost hours of that fateful night in the Whites.

Both Barney and Betty claimed they were captured and taken aboard the aircraft, where they were separated and examined by the grayish humanoids. The captors kept samples of the Hills' hair, fingernails, and skin cells, before depositing them back into their car. The Hills watched the craft depart, and then continued driving south on I-93 in a daze.

It seems far-fetched, sure, but consider this: While she was hypnotized, Betty recalled the humanoid leader showing her a star map of where her captors came from. She drew the star chart from memory during her hypnosis, and it bears a stark resemblance to a true, mapped corner of the galaxy. The twin stars Betty illustrated as the UFO's home base are real—the Zeta Reticuli, a system some 39 light years from Earth—and seemingly impossible to duplicate on paper. Unless you've been personally shown by a native.

DO IT

Because the Hills were chased along US 3 and I-93 through the Whites, there are a ton of options that follow their general path. For a simple hike, bag Cannon Mountain via the Kinsman Ridge Trail in Franconia Notch State Park (trailhead: 44.168083, -71.682747); it's about 2 miles to the 4,040-foot summit. Note the scale of Cannon's famous cliff face—Betty Hill testified that the UFO was at least one and a half times as big when it passed. For a longer circuit that follows the UFO's supposed trajectory, knock out the 16-mile counterclockwise loop that links Franconia Ridge, Cannon Mountain, and Lonesome Lake: From the trailhead (44.111679, -71.681969), take the Liberty Spring Trail east to Franconia Ridge, where you'll continue north. Liberty, Little Haystack, Lincoln, and Lafayette are available for bagging (scan west to see Cannon Mountain, I-93, and possible UFOs). Drop off the ridge on the Greenleaf Trail, which takes you west to the Kinsman Ridge trailhead (above). Climb Cannon, then descend to take the Lonesome Lake Trail to the Lafayette Campground on I-93. From here, walk about 2 miles south along I-93 to close the loop (or take a shuttle or hitch a ride, but be wary of humanoids).

Green with Envy

Killington Peak, Long Trail, Calvin Coolidge State Forest, Vermont

I T'S UNCLEAR why Samuel Peters had such a huge chip on his shoulder, but the man loved to hate Vermont. He was a Connecticut native, and while it's not necessarily rare for New Englanders to dispute which state reigns superior in the region, Peters's contempt wasn't playful. He believed Vermont to be utterly godless, a slice of the colony that was in disarray. So, in 1763, Peters rode into Vermont, believing it was his God-given duty to rescue the area.

At some point, between baptisms and sermons, the reverend found himself on a trek up one of the local high points. Vermonters today know the impulse. There wasn't a trail network at the time, so Peters and his band bushwhacked their way to the top of what's now known as Killington Peak, the "beast of the East" and the state's second-tallest mountain.

It was there, in a moment of weakness, that Peters let Vermont capture his heart, if only briefly. He stood atop the craggy peak and scanned out to the unbroken layers of wooded peaks that seem to melt into the horizon. There was no major ski resort hogging the view, there wasn't any singletrack snaking through the vista—only the most vibrant shade of green. Peters smashed a bottle of whiskey on the pinnacle, christening the land Verd Mont, "a new name worthy of the Athenians and ancient Spartans . . . in token that her mountains and hills shall be ever green, and shall never die."[2]

But the sentimentality wouldn't last. Peters returned to Connecticut and became an outspoken Loyalist sympathizer, defending British interests in America. He eventually fled to England, a vocal supporter of King George III, where he'd pen a defense of Benedict Arnold and a wholly unflattering account of Connecticut's history.

When word reached Peters that the local legislature had convened and declared "Vermont" a new republic in the American colony, he scoffed. "Since Verd Mont became a state in the union with the thirteen states of America, its general assembly have seen proper to change the spelling of Verd-mont, Green Mountain, to that of Ver-mont, Mountain of Maggots," he declared. "Both words are French: And if the former spelling is to give place to the latter, it will prove that the state had rather be considered a mountain of worms than an evergreen mountain!"

It's no wonder Peters was never consecrated after being nominated the Anglican bishop-elect of Vermont shortly thereafter. Peters would continue stirring the pot throughout his life, making more brassy assertions than an election-year politician. He would move back to the States, and eventually, die at the ripe age of ninety, drowning in poverty and, for all intents and purposes, as a cantankerous old man—a characterization his spirit still upholds today.

Hikers report odd sensations of being shoved on the summit of Killington. Some have said that they feel their hair being pulled. The stories are worse just below the summit in the crude Cooper Lodge. Thru-hikers have claimed to see Peters's ghost in the shelter; some have suggested that it pokes and prods them when they try to sleep. The lodge's register is littered with words like, "creepy," "spooky," and "unsettling," which is probably the way Peters would have wanted it.

DO IT

The best way to crest Killy is midway through the 272-mile Long Trail. But, if you don't have three weeks, try this section: From the Appalachian trailhead on US 4 (43.666570, -72.850057), head 5.7 miles south through the land of green mountains to the Cooper Lodge (first-come, first-served), the highest shelter on the Long Trail. Hop onto the summit spur and take it about 0.2 mile to Killington's 4,236-foot pinnacle. Spin-around views stretch into New Hampshire, New York, and even Massachusetts on a clear day. Retrace your steps for a 12-mile out-and-back, or arrange for a shuttle car and keep going roughly 17 miles south on the Long Trail to the parking lot on VT 140 (43.456879, -72.932769) for a 23-mile point-to-point. (Spend the night at any of the handful of lean-tos on this stretch; they are supposedly ghost-free.)

A Small Fortune

Thimble Islands, Long Island Sound,
Branford, Connecticut

THEY SAY the Thimbles off the coast of Connecticut consist of more than 365 islands. That's a slice of paradise every day for more than a year, if you timed your paddles for low tide when the Atlantic reveals more of the granite mounds than have names. They range in size from feet-wide to acres-wide, the archipelago spanning the entire Stony Creek harbor, as though Mother Nature cast her lots across the Long Island Sound, which—in a sense—is what the nefarious Captain Kidd did.

Yes, the pirate made a thing out of terrorizing the aquamarine waters of the Caribbean, but William Kidd was a New Englander, and that's where he'd return. He was born in Scotland sometime in the 1640s, but settled in anglicized New York City. Centuries-old periodicals suggest that he made a go of it—befriending governors and prominent colonials—but, whether for the seventeenth-century strictures or simple boredom, he soon gave it up for a life at sea.

Kidd started off small, apprenticing on a Caribbean-bound ship, but eventually the crew mutinied, and by election or force, he became the new captain of the *Blessed William*. Legend has it that the British governor refused to pay Kidd and his crew wages—so they voluntarily attacked the French to steal enough to make a living. Whether there's actual truth to that or not, it's clear Kidd had a knack for it. He spent the next decade or so plundering ships and port towns and even made somewhat of an honest living as a sort of bounty hunter of the seas, earning some £150 per ship.

It's hard to say why Kidd settled down in 1691, but he did. Seemingly instantaneously, he married a young, twenty-something British woman, moved into a beautiful home with fluted chimneys on the water in New York City, and raised two daughters. He supposedly owned a pew at Trinity Church. It suited him for nearly five years, but, like the song, there was really only ever one sort of life for him: He ditched his family, built up a ship (called *Adventure*, no less), loaded some thirty-four cannons and a crew of 150 men, and set out to wreak havoc on the globe. In the half decade that followed, Captain Kidd is said to have amassed a fortune worth millions in gold, silk, and jewels—which is somewhere in the Thimbles.

See, at some point, the law caught up to Kidd. In an act of desperation, he announced to British authorities that he'd buried his treasure somewhere before leaving the Long Island Sound and he'd give some of his stash to the Royal Crown if they let him off the hook. They didn't bite and the pirate was hanged in London in 1701, his dead body left swaying from the gibbet over the River Thames for more than three years as a sick warning to any would-be marauders who passed through.

And so his riches remain—somewhere. But the tales of the tides that shift just so, covering and uncovering rocks, reefs, and sandbars in the Long Island Sound, have left some to believe that perhaps Kidd still controls these waters.

DO IT

There is no wrong way to do the Thimbles, but launching from Guilford makes for the easiest logistics: Park at the end of Trolley Road (41.258886, -72.704059), and set out in Joshua Cove. Paddle west following the coast past a number of Thimble Islands and pull up wherever suits (so long as it's not private property; a handful of the Thimbles are). Paddling the Long Island Sound will be easier and less choppy than the open ocean, but don't expect lake-style calmness. Do it right and time the tide so the wind is at your back going out and returning. Not comfortable paddling solo? Boat rental shops around Branford also offer guided tours to match skill levels.

The Old Coot

Mt. Greylock, Bellows Pipe Trail, Mt. Greylock State Reservation, Massachusetts

WESTERN MASSACHUSETTS'S Berkshires may be one of the region's most popular vacation destinations today, but they weren't always so. Before the art festivals, the farm-to-table restaurants, and the throngs of leaf-peepers, 3,491-foot Mt. Greylock and the surrounding Taconic Mountains were nothing more than vast farmlands. Settlers flocked to the area for its rich soils, plentiful lakes, and fruitful hunting grounds, and, by the mid-1800s, it was studded with modest farmhouses.

A Yankee named Bill Saunders owned perhaps the most extraordinary farm at the time. Hemmed in by natural ridges, Saunders's farm spanned a wooded hilltop on Greylock's eastern flanks. There, he tended to more than 300 sheep and constructed an extravagant home for his wife, Emma, to raise their children. With the help of some local handymen, she would tend the farm by herself when Bill was forced to leave to fight in the Civil War.

But Bill never returned. In the years that followed, Emma was forced to believe that he had died in action. So when one of the field workers showed romantic interest in her, Emma conceded that she'd be hard-pressed to find another strong, reliable man after the war to help her and married him. The two started a new life on the old farm.

And yet, perhaps she had moved on too quickly.

Years later, a battered and ragged Bill limped back to his farm. He trudged up the path from Adams and through a corridor of fall-gilded hardwoods to his home, his breath smoke drifting skyward in the cool night. He had dreamed of his homecoming since the day he left, years prior, and after all of the battles and the injuries and the gore, the moment was upon him. But when he approached his home, he was startled to hear a mirthful cackle ring from the wooden cabin. Peering through the frosted windows, he saw his old life taking place before his eyes: Emma was laughing as she dished a meal to their children—no longer babies. And another man, young and bearded with a square jaw and thick shoulders, was smiling broadly and clapping his son on the back. "Daddy!" his son squealed, looking up into the bearded man's eyes.

Bill tore himself away from the window, as hot tears rolled down his cheeks. But like any good old Yankee, he had no choice but to pull himself up by his bootstraps. So he left. He built a shack deep in the woods of Mt. Greylock and became a recluse. People began to call him—unkempt and unrecognizable as he was—the Old Coot of Adams. But legend has it that, while he could let his family go, Bill simply couldn't abandon his farm and old livelihood. He'd sneak to his old fields to work them late in the evening when no one could see him. Odder still, though, was that after he passed away, townspeople still reported seeing the Old Coot wandering from Adams up Greylock to the hilltop farm. His ghost was even photographed in local newspapers twice—a dark, blurry mass floating through the woods like a zephyr.

Hikers today still claim to see the spirit of the scruffy Old Coot sneaking to his old farm on the Bellows Pipe Trail, which ascends Greylock from Adams. The area is shrouded in hardwoods today, which is perhaps why the Old Coot is still trying to tend to it.

DO IT

Highpoint Massachusetts via the Bellows Pipe Trail. From the Bernard Farm parking lot at Notch Road (42.673302, -73.139462), it's 5.5 miles to the summit: Pick up the Bellows Pipe Trail south of the reservoir and take it 4.2 miles on the Old Coot's route to a junction. From there, hop on the Appalachian Trail and take it 0.5 mile to the 3,491-foot roof of Massachusetts. Retrace your steps on the return or circle back on the Appalachian and Bernard Farm Trails.

Where Nothing Grows

Mt. Chocorua, Piper Trail, White Mountain National Forest, New Hampshire

THE SUMMIT view on Mt. Chocorua is one of those scenes that outruns your vision. Rows and rows of piercingly green peaks stretch into the horizon in every direction, hiding sparkling lakes and wildflower meadows in their creases. On a clear day, the 360-degree view could convert even the biggest hiking skeptic into a full-blown nature lover.

Pretty as it may be, however, the spin-around vista from Chocorua's exposed summit defies science. In New Hampshire, timber line, the natural boundary where trees stop growing, is estimated around 4,500 feet. It makes sense, then, that the northern Whites, which surpass 5,000 feet tall, are lauded for their long-range views and alpine environments. But Mt. Chocorua rises just 3,475 feet, well below natural timber line. And yet, no trees grow on its bare cone. Consider it a phenomenon—or a curse.

The mountain's namesake was a chief and a prophet in the local tribe centuries ago. Every day, Chocorua would climb to the top of the mountain, clamber through the dense foliage, edge out onto the rocky precipice, and look out over his land. He was imposing in stature, with broad shoulders and deep-set black eyes, and was particularly respected, both among the Native Americans and the settlers. It's said that people knew he was capable of unleashing a fierce temper, but they had never provoked him to do so.

Chocorua had one son, about nine years old, who often visited a young married couple, Cornelius and Caroline Campbell. The Campbells had children of their own, but they were neighborly and enjoyed hosting the young boy, while he reveled in inspecting their refined home and their many effects. One day, the boy discovered a vial of poison, which Cornelius had prepared for a mischievous fox that had long disturbed the settlement. Not knowing what it was, Chocorua's son drank it. He returned home to his father and died that night.

From that moment, Chocorua was consumed with hatred and an unwavering desire for revenge. So when Cornelius left his home to tend the fields one balmy June morning, Chocorua called on the Campbell home and slaughtered Caroline and the children. When Cornelius returned to discover the gruesome murders of his family members, he immediately suspected Chocorua. He pursued the Native American chief up the mountain, through the dense woods, to the rocky bluff where he intended to kill him.

"Throw yourself into the abyss below!"[3] Cornelius cried.

"The Great Spirit gave life to Chocorua, and Chocorua will not throw it away at the command of a white man," Chocorua calmly replied.

"Then hear the Great Spirit speak in the white man's thunder!" Cornelius retorted, pointing his rifle at the chief.

"A curse upon you, white men! May the Great Spirit curse you when he speaks in the clouds, and his words are fire! Chocorua had a son, and you killed him while the sky looked bright! Lightning blast your crops! Wind and fire destroy your dwellings! The Evil Spirit breathe death upon your cattle! Your graves lie in the war path of the Indian! Panthers howl, and wolves fatten over your bones! Chocorua goes to the Great Spirit—his curse stays with the white men!"

It's said that Chocorua died there, on the rocky precipice, and, for all intents and purposes, so did the settlement. The strongest men suffered illness, the cattle died, the crops stopped producing—and gales tore the trees off the mountaintop from their roots.

DO IT

From the trailhead (43.939532, -71.225910) just west of Conway, pick up the Piper Trail and take it 3.5 miles to the exposed scalp of Mt. Chocorua. Emerge from the thick hardwoods near mile 3.3 after gaining some 2,700 feet of elevation; then it's a short walk across slabby rocks to the high point. Retrace your steps on the return.

The Grand Design

Ship Harbor, Ship Harbor Trail,
Acadia National Park, Maine

I N THE mid-1700s, the massive brigantine *Grand Design* set out from Northern Ireland for Philadelphia. It would have been filled with some 200 passengers, young and old, all seeking new life in the New World, be that religious freedom or economic opportunity. But old annals suggest that as the vessel encroached on the eastern seaboard, it faced severe gales. The weather was turning, the winds whipping the summer heat into the season's first frost and driving the *Grand Design* toward the rocky coast. At the mercy of the elements, the 3-ton ship ran aground on an island of pink granite.

It's impossible to know how the island appeared to the emigrants, but if it's at all as it is today, the spruces would have been their usual deep green, blanketing the island down to the water where they mingle with the waves. The tamaracks would be festooned with fall's splendor, shocking the green canopy with yellow. The wildlife would have been active this time of year—otters tumbling through clear water, bald eagles perching on tree limbs, moose munching in the brush. When the sun rose the next day, setting the scene alight, it's not unreasonable to think that the passengers might have tipped their caps: There are worse places to be marooned.

The remaining emigrants—some texts suggest that a handful had died due to illness on the journey overseas—disembarked the *Grand Design* in Ship Harbor at the southwesternmost point of Mt. Desert Island. There was no sign of human life, which we know now was odd. The Wabanaki have inhabited Maine and, specifically, Mt. Desert Island, for thousands of years, but for some reason they weren't present in the mid-1700s, a gap in their history. So the colonists were alone. They devised a plan: Half would remain on the coast and subsist on the land, while the other would venture into the wild to find help, taking with them the remaining supplies from the *Grand Design*.

But the plan failed. Old 1800s-era annals from the town of Warren are clear: Nothing was ever heard of again from the search party. In fact, to this day, no sign of them—even bones, bleak as it sounds—has ever been found. They simply vanished.

As for the others who waited by the shore, they slowly succumbed to starvation or exposure, and their graves (more than ninety of them) supposedly litter the woods east of Ship Harbor. Only six of the original passengers of the *Grand Design* survived winter on Mt. Desert Island before being rescued by passing Native Americans.

Today, the hikes along Ship Harbor are some of the national park's best day trips for solitude, access, and sweat-to-views ratio, but there's a catch: People report feeling uncharacteristically melancholy when walking through the spruce woods, even those who've never heard the story of the *Grand Design*. Others have noted how incredibly famished they feel, even though the hike is less than a mile and a half. Still others have said they've seen an amorphous emaciated man lingering in the shadows. It seems Acadia's beauty can't hide its past.

DO IT

From the trailhead off ME 102A (44.231645, -68.325723) aka Harbor Drive, head south toward the coast on the Ship Harbor Trail. It's a double-loop, or a 1.3-mile figure eight of sorts. Stay west (hiker's right) on the way out to the rosy-pink granite shore to obtain the best vantages over Ship Harbor. On the return, take the easternmost paths (also hiker's right) to explore the woods; keep an eye peeled for unmarked graves.

Home Free

Lakes of the Clouds Hut, Crawford Path, White Mountain National Forest, New Hampshire

WILLIAM CURTIS may have been on the wrong side of sixty, but he had a résumé's worth of marquee peaks to his name. He was solidly built with gamey calves that rippled as he climbed and, at sixty-three, not only was he was still hiking, but he was a contributing member of the acclaimed Appalachian Mountain Club.

On June 30, 1900, the mountaineer planned to tackle 6,288-foot Mt. Washington, the most prominent peak east of the Mississippi. It's an impressive objective, though the ascent isn't technical. The country's oldest maintained foot trail, the Crawford Path, leads hardy hikers 8.5 miles straight to the top. So, beneath midsummer's clear, blue skies, Curtis and his climbing partner, fellow AMC member Allan Ormsbee, set out on the Crawford Path and climbed. But, at some point, the weather turned.

It's not entirely surprising that the conditions went sour on Mt. Washington—they often do. The average temperature on the summit is 27.3 degrees Fahrenheit. The average wind speed is 35 miles per hour. As of press time, the second-highest wind speed ever recorded had occurred on Mt. Washington's cone: 231 miles per hour. Rough math indicates that a 70-miles-per-hour wind would be enough to overcome gravity and lift an average-size human off the ground. Wind of two hundred thirty-one miles per hour is ridiculous.

The station on Mt. Washington's summit only started recording weather data in 1933, so it's impossible to say just how bad the conditions turned on June 30, 1900, but Curtis and Ormsbee never made it to the top. Ormsbee, only twenty-nine years old, was found, days later, his body

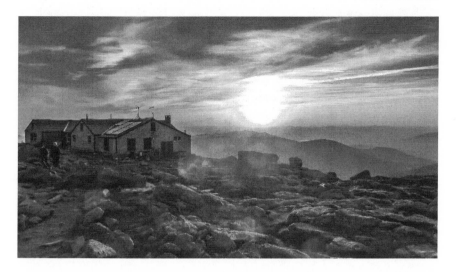

covered in cuts and bruises, just beneath the summit. He was less than a football field away from the crude shelter that could have saved his life. Curtis, meanwhile, was recovered near the Lakes of the Clouds, a tandem of sky-hugging tarns southwest of the summit, beneath 5,372-foot Mt. Monroe. He was roughly 1.5 miles away from the summit shelter and about the same distance from the safety of the trees below; he was caught in a fatal no-man's-land.

A year later, the AMC built an emergency shelter in the col between Monroe and Big Wash—the exact spot Curtis had perished. It would become the Lakes of the Clouds Hut, the AMC's highest shelter and home to at least one disturbed ghost.

After Curtis and Ormsbee succumbed to Big Wash, they were each memorialized where they died. A wooden cross near the Mt. Washington summit marked Ormsbee's final resting place, while a bronze plaque commemorating Curtis was secured to a boulder in the saddle beneath Mt. Monroe. If passing hikers criticize the duo's decision to press on for the summit after the weather turned, an unseen force supposedly pushes them or knocks them down.

The spirit of Curtis, in particular, is so disturbed that he refuses to remain in the col. According to local lore, AMC "croomembers" found Curtis's plaque some years later, detached from the rock, in the threshold of the Lakes of the Clouds hut. They would secure it to the boulder and, again, awake to it sitting in the doorway. This continued, without reason or explanation, until the plaque was bolted to the wall in the crew's staff room inside Lakes of the Clouds Hut, away from the elements—and the wrath of Mt. Washington.

DO IT

You won't find a more legendary tour in the East than the 23-mile Presidential Traverse, which tops eight peaks, including Mt. Washington. It's no cakewalk—it gains more than 10,000 feet of elevation—so set aside two or three days for the epic adventure, starting on the Valley Way Trail off Gorham Hill Road (44.371474, -71.289318) and trekking south to the Crawford trailhead off Mt. Clinton Road (44.223293, -71.411611). If you do the Presi, you'll land at Lakes of the Clouds near mile 13; reserve a bunk at outdoors.org. For a hike that's less of a commitment, start at the Crawford trailhead and head 7 miles north to Lakes of the Clouds. From there, either retrace your steps or keep going about 1.5 miles to the roof of the Whites. Check conditions ahead of time at mountwashington.org (don't push your luck in bad weather), and be sure to tip your cap to the mountaineers before you who haven't been so lucky.

Southeast

An American Haunting

Bell Witch Cave, Cave Tour, Adams, Tennessee

CERTAINLY NO one will ever wish for John Bell's fate for himself, but it would be nice to have been a fly on the wall. His is one of the most told stories in the South and still, no one is quite sure what to make of it.

At the beginning of the nineteenth century, a tide of immigrants flowed from older states along the Atlantic seaboard to the far southwestern frontier. They were generally honest folks, deeply religious, and simple. One such man was Bell, who, at fifty-four, moved his family and eight slaves from North Carolina to Robertson County, Tennessee, 30 miles northwest of Nashville. Bell purchased one of the community's largest homesteads—a log cabin with six rooms—along a horseshoe-bend of the Red River, and began what could have been a very ordinary life, but never was.

He was a smart man who raised his children with as good an education as could be found in the area and was purportedly a man of great integrity. He became a deacon in his local church and treated his slaves well enough that multiple periodicals from the time mention as much.

But things turned in 1817, when Bell and his family began hearing weird noises in and around their home. For instance, there would be rapping on the door, and yet, when answered, no one was there. There were beatings on the walls and scratching on the floorboards, and, still, no explanation. The children began waking up in the middle of the night suggesting that something—or someone—was gnawing on their bedposts. At some point, Bell and his wife began hearing smacking lips and sharp inhaling, but could find no source.

It's impossible to say what Bell was thinking at the time, but he didn't really act until his youngest daughter, Betsy, began waking in the night shouting that she was being beaten. Red welts and blue bruises supported her claims, and John Bell had had enough. He confessed the goings-on to a trustworthy neighbor, James Johnson, who, although not ordained, was prominent in the church. Johnson was a good man and didn't question his friend. He prayed earnestly over the Bell family and even opted to spend the night. But it wasn't enough. The voice returned raucous as ever. Knowing full well that reputations were at stake, Johnson and the Bells agreed to keep the ghost a secret until they could figure out how to eradicate the thing.

But, as Irvin S. Cobb eloquently put it in 1922, "to maintain secrecy in a case like this was as utterly impossible a task as trying to bottle up a cyclone in a cider jug. Immediately tales of the things that were happening beneath the roof of the Bells spread through the whole countryside."[4] Eventually, visitors—including Gen. Andrew Jackson—were traveling to the Bells' home from near and far to witness the malice of the unseen invader for themselves.

For reasons unknown, the Bells continued to live with the force, now referred to as the Bell Witch. Some people speculated that the ghost, whose voice had supposedly become clearer and clearer over time, was the spirit of Kate Batts, an eccentric old woman who lived a few miles from the Bells' homestead. She and Bell had gotten into a dispute about land at some point, and, as she was seemingly the only person he'd ever butted heads with[5], she quickly became suspect number one. Others believed the ghost was unrelated to anyone Bell had had dealings with in his lifetime, and still others believed it was a hoax. But three years after Bell started hearing voices, he was poisoned to death. His family found him reclining in the sitting room, cold as ice, beside a vial of unidentified liquid, as the voice purportedly proclaimed, "I gave ol' Jack a big dose of that last night, which fixed him!"

But, oddly, the end of John Bell didn't spell the end for the Bell Witch, who continued terrorizing members of the Bell family and Red River community into the next century. The area's annals are littered with old accounts of people facing similar hardships as John Bell did, and to this day, no one is sure why. "Either all the residents of a sizable community were the simultaneous victims of a monstrous hallucination, alike affecting men and women of varying natures and continuing without abatement for over two years," Cobb postulated. "Or, a marvelous master of trick and device, for no apparent reason or possible personal gain, succeeded through a period of months and years in practicing a monumental deception without once being caught in the act...

... Or, what, to the average individual today seems most incredible of all, that the Bell Witch was a disembodied spirit of malice and cruelty, possessing unearthly faculties for mischief, memory, divination, and malignity."

DO IT

As if this tale isn't creepy enough, the only aspect of the Bell homestead that remains is a subterranean tunnel believed to be 15 miles deep. John Bell owned it in the early 1800s and, while not necessarily fundamental to the story, some people suggest that it's where the Bell Witch remains. Since it's still private property, you must go on a guided tour (bellwitchcave.com) to explore it. Find the cave at 430 Keysburg Rd. (36.590749, -87.060739). Yes, *The Blair Witch Project* and *An American Haunting* are based, in part, off this legend.

Ghost Lights

Table Rock Mountain, Mountains-to-Sea Trail,
Linville Gorge Wilderness, North Carolina

MONG THE scads of peaks called "Brown Mountain" across the globe, perhaps none was more appropriately named than the one nestled in the fringes of Pisgah National Forest. It's technically part of the postcard-worthy Blue Ridge Mountains, but that seems like a cartographer's joke. Lost amid folds of nondescript, forgettable hillocks, this Brown Mountain is less a peak than a ridgeline, barely surpassing 2,700 feet. Like the mounds and creases around it, Brown Mountain is wholly unremarkable—until nighttime.

For more than 800 years, people have reported seeing floating orbs of light crest the ridge and snake between the oaks and hickories. And, for more than 800 years, people have been stumped. The Cherokee believed the lights were lanterns, the spirits of maidens searching for their men who were lost in a fierce twelfth-century battle with the Catawba warriors. Geology seems to favor this theory: Look at a satellite image of Brown Mountain—which the Native Americans couldn't do, of course—and you'll see, clearly, that the Wilson creekbed east of the ridge forms the profile of a chief looking to the battlefield.

Seems far-fetched, sure, which is probably why geologists in the early 1900s contended that the lights were those of locomotives. But when the tracks washed away with a massive flood in 1916, the lights remained. Others suggested swamp gas, a phenomenon where chemical reactions common in marshes create a sort of luminescent green hue—but there are no swamps in the area. Other ideas, like foxfire, radium, moonshine stills, and geological anomalies, were all disproved. UFOs and aliens were in vogue as an explanation at one time, but—predictably—that, too, was never confirmed. Perhaps the easiest explanation has been that the orbs are car headlights, or at least the reflections of them. But that hardly explains the existence of the lights before the twentieth century.

With no consensus, perhaps it's worth considering the original explanation: At night, the ghosts of Cherokee women comb Brown Mountain by torchlight in search of lost warriors.

DO IT

There are a number of overlooks scattered along the Blue Ridge Parkway that offer a long-range view of Brown Mountain (Wiseman's View, Brown Mountain Light Overlook, and Green Mountain Overlook, to name a few), but the best vista is from Table Rock Mountain's distinct summit. Do it as a day hike: From the Table Rock Parking Lot (35.886572, -81.884781), take the Table Rock Summit Trail 0.7 mile to the 4,101-foot plateau. Do it as a weekend: Loop 22 miles counterclockwise from the Wolf Pit trailhead (35.823981, -81.889783), stringing together the Wolf Pit, Mountains-to-Sea, Spence Ridge, and Linville Gorge Trails. You'll pass the Table Rock Summit Trail spur near mile 7.4. (Spend night one near the Chimneys around mile 6.3 and night two along the Linville River in the gorge around mile 13.) From the Table Rock summit, scan east at nightfall to Brown Mountain; the flickering lights are roughly the size of a basketball from the looker's perspective.

Lover's Leap

Noccalula Falls, Historic Gorge Trail, Noccalula Park, Alabama

NOCCALULA FALLS is no delicate ribbon of sparkling water. The torrent is nearly as wide as it is tall, a 90-foot fireworks blast of a cascade amid Black Creek, with mist that billows skyward like plumes of smoke, engulfing the jade basin below. It's so arresting, mystical even, that some of the earliest inhabitants to the area even believed its spray could heal earthly ailments. Maybe that's why the waterfall's namesake jumped.

The daughter of a powerful Cherokee chief, Princess Noccalula was known across the land for her kindness and beauty. While many gallant suitors competed for her hand, it was a young, handsome Cherokee brave who won her heart. But Princess Noccalula's father wanted her to marry a Creek chief, which would both set her up well and unify two warring tribes. Noccalula pleaded with her father to let her marry her love, but he disregarded her, saying she was foolish. With that, he arranged for Noccalula to wed a wealthy Creek warrior who had many horses and many possessions.

On her wedding day, however, Noccalula ran away to the waterfall near her village, a 90-foot cataract fed by Black Creek. Standing on its lip, poised above the violent whirlpool, she vowed she could never marry the Creek chief. Then, she leapt into the curtain of water and plummeted to her death.

Whether she sought to simply end it right then and there or cure her broken heart in the healing waters, Noccalula's spirit was never satisfied. Some visitors claim to have seen her in the gorge, weeping for her lost love. Stare into the mist, and among the swirls, you can see her, too. But be wary of the unexplained forces, and resist the urge to jump.

DO IT

You can visit Noccalula Falls any time of year, but time it for winter or spring when runoff is at its height. From the parking lot (34.042049, -86.021166), pick up the 1.4-mile Historic Gorge Trail, an easy loop that plunges into the chasm and even passes behind the curtain of water (beware the slick walkway). The best vantage of the falls is from right above (a negligible walk from the parking lot), where a statue commemorates the princess—and where she leapt.

Bloody Ed Watson

Watson's Place, Chatham River, Everglades National Park, Florida

O N A map, the tip of Florida is a solid line. On one side, there's solid green, and on the other, an expanse of baby blue. And yet nothing could be further from the truth. At some point, that solid green gives way to the blue—but not all the way—in a tangle of land and water. In real life, the copper-colored tannic drink courses through a maze of hundreds of islands and sandbars, oyster reefs and mangroves, until the wild swamp simply melts into the turquoise ocean. Strong gusts and tidal currents constantly change the lay of the land—which is no doubt why it's where Florida's most prolific serial killer hid out.

Edgar Watson had a handful of murders to his name, including quite possibly one Belle Starr, when he fled to the Florida coast. There, in what's now known as the Ten Thousand Islands region, he commandeered a 40-acre key that the area's first inhabitants had made of shells. The history is fuzzy, but Watson allegedly ran stolen goods from Key West to make enough money to hire a staff to tend a sugarcane plantation on his island. But, legend has it, the man was greedy. At some point, Watson grew tired of paying his farmhands and, instead, took to murdering them on payday. He'd bury them and replace them before anyone realized what kind of business he was running.

The foundation and remnants of Watson's homestead remain today on his island off the Chatham River, and it's unclear just how many corpses are hidden in its shell-choked soil. A pile of crumbling bricks secures a rusty basin of scum-topped water where the outlaw evaporated sugarcane, while vines curl through the foundation's blocks, slowly taking over. And yet, there is a designated campsite at this very spot where paddlers can spend the night. Even creepier, some paddlers claim that Watson himself remains on the island—arguably because he was so unceremoniously kicked off.

While townspeople surely assumed Watson was behind the trouble that plagued South Florida at the time, they didn't have physical evidence to support a conviction—and, most likely, they couldn't find him in the watery labyrinth, anyway. So one day in 1910, when a passing storm revealed the remains of a young woman who was known to have been working on the Watson sugarcane plantation, the locals knew they had their shred of evidence. They waited on the mainland for the sound of Watson's boat firing down the channel, and when he pulled up, they met him with lead.

DO IT

The only way to truly explore the Ten Thousand Islands' liquid horizons is by boat: Launch from the boat ramp in Everglades City (25.845762, -81.387090) and create a loop that suits your time frame. A good bet: Link Chokoloskee Bay, Wilderness Waterway, Rabbit Key Pass, the Gulf of Mexico, Chatham River, and inland bays into a 50-mile loop. Make sure to tag Chatham River in your route-planning; Watson's Place is on the western banks (practice alligator safety). Expert navigators only.

The Phantom Dog

Hutcheson Compound, Ghost House Trail, Big Ridge State Park, Tennessee

TAKE A walk in Big Ridge State Park and it's easy to see why nineteenth-century pioneers settled the area. By the mid-1800s, its medley of old-growth hardwoods, limestone hollows, and wildflower-studded meadows were dotted with homesteads. But it wouldn't last.

Families started leaving, one by one. Local lore has it that ghost activity was to blame, which explains why, by the late 1800s, only one prominent family remained: the Hutchesons. Their confidence in these woods wouldn't save them from the strange occurrences that characterized the area, though. Young Mary Hutcheson contracted tuberculosis before long. As the legend goes, family friends were walking up the wooded path on a particularly dark night to visit the sick girl when they heard an agitated hound barking and howling. They lifted their lanterns, but could see no dog. Around the time Mary's visitors were searching for the hound they'd never find, Mary passed away from her consumption.

The patriarch of the Hutcheson family, Maston, was apparently driven mad by his despair, but still refused to leave the area. He eventually died in 1910, maybe of natural causes—or maybe by the phantom dog.

Today, hikers in the area claim to hear the panting of an approaching dog around the Hutcheson homestead ruins. There's even an unusual case of a visitor's German shepherd refusing to go near the area, setting his feet and baring his teeth, though his owner did not see anything out of the ordinary.

Whatever Maston's cause of death, his spirit is purportedly still restless, haunting visitors who hike through the park to his gravestone—and even appearing in their photos.

DO IT

See both the Hutcheson homestead ruins and the cemetery where Maston was buried on the 1.2-mile, aptly named Ghost House Trail. Begin at the Gristmill trailhead (36.247087, -83.924764) and quickly turn north (hiker's right) onto the trail to complete the loop. If two creepy relics aren't enough, tack on the 2.6-mile Indian Rock Trail, where a plaque marks the site where a settler was ambushed and scalped in 1794.

Craters in the Earth

Carolina Bays, Palmetto Trail, Francis Marion National Forest, South Carolina

MARSHLANDS ARE so prevalent in South Carolina that you might be led to believe the whole state is just one big lowland swamp. But if you look at a satellite image of the Lower 48, you'll get a different picture. Small, ovular depressions pepper the East Coast, as though it was sprayed with bullets. There are roughly half a million of the craters across the seaboard, and an unusually high concentration in South Carolina. More often than not, the state's wetland habitats are contained within the dimples.

No one seemed to notice the egg-shaped depressions until 1700, when a colonial explorer wrote that he and his crew had plodded through "a prodigious wide and deep swamp"[6] and were "forced to strip stark-naked and much ado to save ourselves from drowning." Further, no one seemed to care until the 1930s when black-and-white aerial photos revealed deciduous vegetation and farmlands pockmarked with craters. And, more than 80 years after *that*, we still don't understand them.

Here's what we know: They vary in size from tiny to massive, but they're all elliptical, each one's major axis stretching from the northwest to the southeast. They tend to have raised rims of sand on the southeast ends, and they're biodiverse hot spots, where ancient species like longleaf pines and rare ones like tiny sedges thrive. They're often trimmed with bay trees (which is why they're called "bays").

Humans have wrecked most of the bays, but handfuls remain across the Atlantic seaboard, including a few hundred in South Carolina. From those, scientists have postulated a number of theories as to their origins, each more absurd than the last. The earliest scientists suggested that a shower of meteorites created the depressions, but no one could produce a single stone as evidence to support the claim. Others offered wind or erosion, but couldn't explain why the process didn't affect the rest of the country. Then people got exceedingly creative: Some suggested that ancient schools of fish created the depressions in which to spawn when a shallow sea covered much of the country. Another suggested dust devils and another bear-size, prehistoric beavers. Some considered that the depressions were scars from ancient icebergs that grounded and melted out millennia ago. Each one was disproved.

Right now, there are two leading theories. One: When the earth was covered in a sheet of ice some 13,000 years ago, a comet that was unusually small and unusually slow exploded just before colliding with the Northern Hemisphere, shedding shards across the ice. This theory needs work, of course, and the timing may not even be right, according to some scientists' formulas. Two: Something beyond our comprehension, be it cosmic or otherworldly, is to blame. Oddly, the latter seems the most plausible at this point.

DO IT

You can see Carolina bays all along the Atlantic seaboard, but there are roughly two dozen that are preserved in the Francis Marion National Forest, so try the 47-mile Fox Passage section of the Palmetto Trail that bisects it. Do it as a thru-hike, linking the Awendaw trailhead (33.037333, -79.617410) with the one just south of Bonneau (33.278461, -79.962215). The bays aren't always obvious; some have drained. Keep your eyes peeled for wetland habitat. The Palmetto Trail skirts a bunch and crosses some via boardwalks in this section. Hikers have reported the feeling of being watched here—which, if theory two holds true, isn't all that surprising. For a shorter hike, do an out-and-back from the Awendaw (eastern) trailhead. You'll cross a Carolina bay in the first 5 miles.

The Spearfinger

Noland Creek, Noland Creek Trail, Great Smoky Mountains National Park, North Carolina

WITH MORE than 150 cemeteries peppering the Smokies' high-elevation balds, blue ridges, and lush gorges, it seems almost arbitrary to whittle down the material to one ghost story. But it's a good one—one that melds both Cherokee legend and real-life happenstance.

The Cherokees believed that a terrible ogress lived in the Smokies. She could assume any human form or appearance to suit her purposes, and—because her purpose was often to feast on small children—that was frequently that of a tender, grandmotherly woman. Despite the shape-shifter's fragile appearance, though, her skin was always impenetrable and hard as stone. She could not succumb to human weapons. The one giveaway as to her devilish spirit was her right hand, which bore a long, awl-like forefinger made of obsidian, by which she stabbed unsuspecting children. The Cherokee called her Spearfinger.

As the legend goes, Spearfinger would assume her grandmotherly appearance and drift down from the ridges to troll the trails north of Lake Fontana where children were berry picking. "Come, my grandchildren," she would say, enticing them to come close to her. She'd prop the unsuspecting children on her lap as though she were going to comb their hair and then pierce them in the backs with her spear-like finger.

The area north of Lake Fontana is flecked with trails today—we could recommend one, tell you to watch your children, and call it good. But, for better or worse, the oddities don't end there. There's another story, that of an old settler whose daughter went missing near Noland Creek, north of

Lake Fontana. Whether you believe it was the doing of Spearfinger or not, the stories agree on what happened next: The father went into a frenzy. Panicked, he set out to track his missing daughter and bring her home. When he ventured into the deep, dark woods near Noland Creek, he was ambushed and murdered by Natives.

Today, hikers have reported seeing a floating white light in the area around Lower and Upper Noland Cemeteries, not unlike a lantern. Some people suggest that it's the spirit of the settler still searching for his daughter. Others say he leads lost hikers back to safety. It seems prudent to remind you here, though, that Spearfinger is a shapeshifter.

DO IT

Pick up the Noland Creek Trail from the trailhead on Lakeview Drive (35.456638, -83.526120) and head as far as you'd like north, paralleling Noland Creek away from Lake Fontana. Find the spur for the lower cemetery near mile 2.8 on hiker's left. You'll pass the upper cemetery near mile 4.4 on hiker's right. Do it as a day hike or tent at Backcountry Camp 65 or 64 en route (or keep going to 63).

Black Caesar

Elliott Key, Spite Highway,
Biscayne National Park, Florida

BLACK CAESAR may have been duped once, but he was sure it would never happen again. He sat in shackles, trapped in a ship's hold, destined for present-day Florida, his mind racing with ideas for how to possibly escape. A war chieftain in West Africa, he had accrued riches—and a reputation—in a decade of wreaking havoc. He was huge, nearly seven-feet tall, with a massive barrel chest and arms larger than most men's thighs. In Africa, he had embraced his stature, the sort of man who walked with his chin in the air, peering down at everyone he crossed through the bottoms of his eyelids. But he had been lured onto a slave trader's ship by a man showing off watches, silks, and jewels. And now he found himself in a situation that his size couldn't overcome.

But while it was his size that was most reputed, Caesar was also keenly intelligent. And so he befriended one of the ship's mates. He was kind and tender in his veneer of innocence, and it earned him larger meals and a more enjoyable voyage for sure, but Caesar's plan really shone when a tropical hurricane swept through the Atlantic. The storm wrecked the ship among the coral reefs of South Florida, tossing Caesar, shackled, into the torrential waves. Of all of the trapped slaves, it was Caesar whom the mate opted to save. The two then paddled to a cluster of mangroves and waited out the storm.

Mangroves are one of those acts of nature that seem to defy science, tilting the axis of what we know to be true. They grow in tangles of roots and greenery on top of the ocean, like misplaced jungles—soil, sunlight, and air not required. Small marine organisms hide amid their roots and seabirds breed and nest amid their greenery, both of which are so dense, no predators can penetrate—which is probably why this mangrove island ended up being a strategic spot for an aspiring pirate to get his start.

From the tiny mangrove island, just south of present-day Elliott Key, Caesar and his companion could spy the surrounding shipping lanes without being seen. When an unsuspecting ship would pass, the two buccaneers would paddle out on a raft made of mangrove branches and attack. They'd plunder the vessel and then disappear into the mangroves, as if by magic.

The two made a go of it for a while, and even expanded their base to include 7-mile-long Elliott Key, which they turned into a compound of sorts. Legend has it that Caesar imprisoned more than one hundred women on the key and it was, in fact, a woman who tore the friends apart; Caesar is said to have murdered the mate who saved him to solely possess one of the prisoners. It's unclear how Caesar killed his accomplice, but it probably wasn't humane. Caesar's go-to method of murder involved chaining his victim to a rock below the high-tide line, so he or she would slowly drown as the surf crept up the beach. Sometimes, the pirate would strap his victim between two wooden boards and saw him in half—lengthwise.

It's impossible to say whether or not Caesar's lifestyle was sustainable or if he could have established a kingdom of sorts in Biscayne Bay, but he would be outsmarted one more time: Drawn by fame and fortune, he eventually abandoned his harem to join forces with the notorious Blackbeard. Caesar was a lieutenant on the *Queen Anne's Revenge* when he was caught by colonial authorities. He'd have no opportunity to return to South Florida to hide or otherwise leave instructions to anyone regarding his riches before he was publicly hanged in Virginia—which means it's all still there for the taking.

DO IT

Sometime after Black Caesar died, the mangrove island he commandeered would be named "Caesar Rock" on topographic maps. The channel between Elliott Key and Caesar Rock would be called "Caesar Creek." The best way to explore the mangrove-fringed shorelines of the keys is by boat: From the Convoy Point launch (25.463602, -80.334128), paddle roughly 8.5 miles straight east across the channel to dock in the Elliott Key harbor (25.453508, -80.196911). (You can also take a commercial ferry to this point.) From the harbor, link the hiking loop with Spite Highway, a path that travels the length of the key. Take it about 4.5 miles to Elliott Key's southernmost point, where you can look across the channel to Caesar Rock. Camping on Elliott is permitted at the campground, if you choose to spend the night.

Love to Death

Petit Jean Mountain, Winthrop P. Rockefeller Boy Scout Trail, Petit Jean State Park, Arkansas

L
OCALS AROUND this part of the country love the story about Petit Jean so much, they named an entire state park after her. Because, while Petit Jean translates from French to "Little John," the folktale actually concerns a beautiful, green-eyed French girl. And that's exactly the allure.

She was a peasant living in France in the 1700s and her name was Adrienne Dumont. She was in love with a nobleman, called Chavet, and the two were set to be married, which, given their respective social classes, would have been quite a coup for the time. The plan was for Chavet to visit the New World on an expedition for the king, and then wed Adrienne on his return. He refused to marry her beforehand, saying the journey would be long and dangerous and, as much as he loved her, the thought of leaving her a destitute widow was too much for him to bear. And so Adrienne was forced to wait while Chavet ventured to explore the Louisiana Territory.

But that didn't sit well with Adrienne, so she cut her hair, recovered some men's clothes, and conned her way onto Chavet's ship as a cabin boy. She told the other sailors her name was Jean and quickly became known as "Petit Jean" because of her stature. They sailed across the Atlantic, then linked the Mississippi and Arkansas Rivers, ultimately docking at the foot of a mountain in the fringes of Arkansas's Ozarks.

The French crew made nice with the Native Americans, and the legend paints a picture of friendship, peace, and discovery. They lived alongside each other atop the sprawling, limestone massif, overlooking the Arkansas River Valley, before Chavet contracted a terrible illness. Plagued by a fever and convulsions, Chavet drifted in and out of delirium. The Natives desperately tried to nurse him back to health, but his prospects were grim. Adrienne spent each day tending to her love and hoping against odds that he would recover. At some point, Chavet came to just enough to notice his cabin boy's piercingly green eyes. He knew at once that Petit Jean was his Adrienne and, as the tale goes, the hope of everlasting love healed his illness.

Unfortunately, the story doesn't end there. Instead of marrying and beginning a life and family in the New World, the two were torn apart by circumstances again. In a twist of fate, Adrienne succumbed to Chavet's illness almost immediately after the man healed. She was buried atop the sprawling, 2,440-foot mountain where the crew and Natives had settled and Chavet was forced to return home to France without a fianceé, a wife, or hope.

Later, it's said, when people discovered this slice of canyon-riddled wilderness between the Ozarks and Ouachitas, and they set about protecting it, they found an unnatural mound of earth: Adrienne's final resting place atop the large plateau remained. And, apparently, so did her spirit. Today, hikers have reported seeing her ghost wandering atop the craggy mountain that bears her pseudonym in search of long-lost love.

DO IT

First, visit Petit Jean's grave at Stout's Point at the terminus of Stout's Point Road (35.127947, -92.839784). Nab a bird's-eye view over the Arkansas River, more than 1,000 feet below, then head over to the Winthrop P. Rockefeller Boy Scout Trail. From the Mather Lodge (35.117598, -92.937959), the path connects a majority of the park's foot trails into a 12-mile circuit past overlooks, waterfalls, caves, and historic CCC structures.

Lost Paradise

Okefenokee Swamp, Suwannee River, Okefenokee National Wildlife Refuge, Georgia

A FLEET OF courier canoes floated lazily through a cluster of lily pads, clunking off roots in the narrow channel. Cypress trees crowded the blackwater canal, drapes of Spanish moss dangling from their branches like curtains. Curious animals, like black bears, gray foxes, and white-tailed deer, peeked from behind tupelo trunks and saw palmettos. But the red-coated men couldn't see the beauty of it all. They were entranced, on a mission to find the elusive Lost Paradise, an alleged enchanted island where a mysterious tribe of dark-eyed women lived.

The Spanish explorers weren't the first to push north through the swamplands on the present-day state line between Florida and Georgia in search of Lost Paradise. Creek legends tell of other unfortunate souls who either failed to find the island or, worse, died in trying. It was portrayed as a Garden of Eden, a place where streams of crystal-clear water coursed, colorful flowers bloomed year-round, and game was plentiful—a place whose beauty was only surpassed by the women who lived there. Though Lost Paradise was supposedly shrouded in mist and protected by a network of ever-changing, impossible-to-map channels, the conquistadors set out to find its colony of beautiful, dark-eyed swamp women anyway.

As their canoes bumped through the coffee-colored water, the Spanish explorers soon grew drowsy. According to legend, they were so dizzy they could no longer navigate, collapsing into sleep one by one, their boats piling together in a standstill in the quiet swamp.

A day passed, and as the men slowly began opening their eyes to the swamp's hazy mist, they saw several of the most radiant women they had ever seen. The dames glowed and had lovely, musical voices and sweet, angelic faces. Their personalities matched their beauty, and they brought the conquistadors to their island to nurse them back to health. It's unclear how much time the Spaniards spent on Lost Paradise, but when the men were healed, they awoke in their camp with no recollection of how they'd returned.

But the legend doesn't end there, because the men were not satisfied with their taste of Lost Paradise. They headed back out into the murky maze of the Okefenokee to find the island again. Whether they stumbled upon it or succumbed to the swamp, we'll never know, but they never returned. People have since claimed to see lithe forms flitting through the shadows of the massive cypresses and hear soft laughter reverberating through the wetlands, but no one has caught a glimpse of Lost Paradise—and lived to describe it.

DO IT

Today, the Okefenokee remains as rugged and wild as it likely was in the sixteenth century, so the only way to truly explore the liquid labyrinth is by boat. Do it as an overnight: Launch from Kingfisher Landing (30.827873, -82.361155) and link the flatwater of the Suwannee and Middle Fork Suwannee Rivers 5.5 miles east and north to a signed, narrow channel. Then, head 3.3 miles east into the blackwater to Floyds Island, where you can spend the night in a simple, metal-roofed hunting cabin (recreation.gov). Bring gaiters to explore the 5-mile-long island by foot, and keep your eyes peeled for maidens. At night, listen for barred owls and soft laughter. Retrace your strokes to the launch.

Devil's Backbone

Tupelo Swamp, Natchez Trace National Scenic Trail, Canton, Mississippi

THE THICK-CROWNED cypress and tupelos along the Natchez Trace may be pretty during the day, but the giants take a new aura when night falls. They hide in their own shadows, towering above the murky waters and peeking through the silvery mist, playing tricks on your mind. Every so often, a moonbeam catches one, illuminating it from behind like the shadow of a sinister titan. It's enough to unnerve any hiker, and, two centuries ago, any traveler.

The Natchez Trace was a game trail before it was a footpath, a route blazed by large mammals like bison and deer coming up from the Mississippi River to the salt licks of modern-day Nashville, Tennessee. The Chickasaw and Choctaw would use it and further develop it, so by the time President Thomas Jefferson was lobbying for western expansion, peddlers and preachers were using it to connect the eastern states to the trading ports in Mississippi and Louisiana. But no one wanted to be caught on the Natchez Trace after dark.

After floating goods down the Ohio and Mississippi Rivers to markets in Natchez and New Orleans, boatmen (called Kaintucks) would sell their barges for lumber and set out to walk the 450 miles back to Nashville on the Trace. These men were rough and unscrupulous, often hiding behind the giant trees and ambushing innocent traders and plying their booty. Some of the country's most notorious outlaws and serial killers—the Harpe brothers, Samuel Mason, and John Murrell to name a few—got their starts here. They hid out in the swamps of the Trace from the mid-1780s through the 1830s, terrorizing commuters and often killing them in

cold blood. More than 10,000 Kaintucks traveled the Trace at its peak. In that time, hundreds of innocent people simply disappeared from the treed corridor, never to be seen again.

It was the advent of the steamboat that ultimately ended the Wild West nature of the Old Trace, which would become known as the "Devil's Backbone." But while Kaintucks are a thing of the past, the dark corridors have retained their creepiness. Hikers today report a feeling of being watched, while some sense that the forest itself, with its low-hanging branches and tendrils of Spanish moss, reaches out to pull you into the blackwater where so many dead bodies were dumped before.

DO IT

If you want to visit the watery grave, we recommend the short, 0.4-mile loop through the swamplands of Black Lake, west of Pearl River. Parking is easy, right off the Natchez Trace Parkway (32.579673, -89.869774), and the route takes you past tupelos to classic bottomland views. Practice gator safety, and beware the darkness, no matter what time of day you go.

The Curse of the Calusa

Pine Island, Calusa Heritage Trail, Florida
Museum of Natural History, Florida

B ETWEEN THE mangroves and the Calusa mounds, there are so many patches of land off the western coast of Florida that it's generally impossible to chalk young Rommie David Taylor's story up to anything other than fate. Because sometime in 1969, the fourteen-year-old boy stumbled upon a small, man-made key. It was wholly unremarkable—one of thousands just like it—rising some twenty feet out of the tannic water and blanketed with whelk shells.

David, the boy was called, was an industrious kid, somewhat introverted. Old periodicals suggest that he rather embraced his southwest Florida heritage and spent his spare time studying the Calusa Indians who were thriving in the Everglades long before the Spanish arrived in the sixteenth century. For thousands of years, the Calusa prospered, subsisting by hunting and gathering, and it's their elaborate pyramids of shells that today provide the physical framework for the Ten Thousand Islands chain.

Their history is strewn with tales of conquest and wealth, but there was one particular story that fascinated David. It was the tale of a powerful Calusa chief known as Carlos among the missionaries. Carlos was self-assured, a natural leader, who was ultimately executed by the Spanish for being intractable. There's a fantastical narrative about Carlos laying a curse over the Spaniards as the axe fell that would have captured any young boy's imagination, but it became the fabric of David's. The boy became obsessed with Carlos and the Calusas, believing Carlos was likely buried with his treasures and gold somewhere off the coast of southwest Florida.

So when David and his little brother landed upon an old Calusa shell midden in 1969, they grabbed shovels and started digging, as they always had. It's possible David's actions were premeditated, part of an elaborate archaeological investigation, but it seems more likely that the kid was just having fun, lost in his own fantasy of Indians, conquest, and buried treasure. When he struck something hard and unearthed a preserved rib cage that was housing a gold medallion, pure luck seems the most logical explanation. The piece of treasure was like something from the movies (and likely inspired some, anyway), 2.5 inches wide, engraved with symbols and pictures, and inexplicably powerful.

Time passed, and the boy grew anxious. He was increasingly obsessed with the pendant and yet started to believe that what he'd done was wrong—that he had exhumed a skeleton from an ancient burial ground. He couldn't concentrate on his schoolwork and couldn't sleep. He began suffering horrific nightmares, and, eventually, his mother did, too. And then David hit his breaking point: In February 1970, the boy hanged himself from a tree.

His wouldn't be the only tragedy begat by the medallion. The piece of gold allegedly traded hands throughout the decades that followed, people either scamming it from one another or voluntarily surrendering it because of its hold. It seems obvious: The medallion was meant to stay in southwest Florida. And until it's returned, perhaps Chief Carlos's curse hangs over all of us.

DO IT

The Calusa flourished throughout southwest Florida until the eighteenth century, and you can see evidence of their culture all over. Your best bet is to arrange a paddle trip through the Ten Thousand Islands (see page 42-Ed Watson for a possible itinerary), but if you prefer to walk, tackle the 0.7-mile Calusa Heritage Trail from the Randall Research Center (near 26.661425, -82.153283) at the Florida Museum of Natural History's Pine Island campus. The path wends past Calusa canals and shell mounds.

Cold Heart

Mollies Ridge Shelter, Appalachian Trail, Great Smoky Mountains National Park, Tennessee

TEMPERATURE SWINGS in the Smokies are themselves the stuff of legend. Hikers regale each other with stories of wearing shorts and SPF 30 in the valleys, only to encounter subfreezing windchills and even snow when they reach the higher-elevation balds. It makes sense: The lowlands in the Great Smoky Mountains hover around 800 feet of elevation, and yet Clingmans Dome, the park high point, soars to more than 6,600 feet. A lot can happen in the miles between.

Hikers, though, certainly weren't the first to be mystified by the Smokies' confusion of seasons. That honor likely belongs to Mollie, a young Cherokee woman who lived in the area long before Benton MacKaye first dreamed up the Appalachian Trail. Mollie was in love with a handsome Cherokee warrior, called White Eagle. Legend has it that one day, White Eagle didn't return from a hunting trip. Mollie hung around for a while, but paranoia consumed her and she couldn't fathom a life without her lover. And so she set out to find him. She combed the ridge that today forms the national park's backbone and the natural state line between Tennessee and North Carolina, looking for any signs of White Eagle.

The story doesn't tell us whatever happened to White Eagle, but we know that at some point, as is wont to happen in the Smokies, the weather turned. A blizzard stormed through, shrouding the Cherokee trail network and blanketing the landscape in white. It persisted for days, and, in an ironic twist, Mollie herself never returned home. Later, she was found at an intersection of ridges beneath a canopy of beeches. She had frozen to death.

DO IT

From the parking lot in Fontana Dam (35.453751, -83.809181), it's about 10 miles to Mollies Ridge Shelter (first-come, first-served). Thru-hikers have reported seeing a hazy shadow of the hut's namesake scouring the area nearby for her lost love. If you catch a glimpse, be sure to invite her inside the three-walled shelter; it's believed she haunts those who don't offer to help. From there, you can retrace your steps, or keep going about 29 miles north to Newfound Gap (35.611183, -83.425285).

The Voodoo Queen

Manchac Swamp, Pass Manchac, Manchac Wildlife Management Area, Louisiana

OLD AUNT Julia Brown was not a woman to be crossed. A descendant of West African slaves down in Cajun country, she surely had a reason to be angry, but that woman had a mean streak. She lived alone in a shack at the edge of the bayou and would sit on her porch, rocking in her chair and mumbling under her breath in Creole or singing made-up songs. An old *Times-Picayune* article quotes the refrain of one: "One day I'm gonna die, and I'm gonna take you all with me."

Weirder: Aunt Julia supposedly practiced voodoo, not necessarily pins-in-dolls stuff, but she possessed some sort of otherworldly power and could heal the sick and foretell the future. And someone who can heal the sick and foretell the future surely is capable of cursing other people, or so the townspeople believed.

And yet, whether by spiritual healing, fortune-telling, or pure luck, the old dingbat managed to somehow amass a fortune. At one point, she owned a vast majority of the property around Frenier Beach, a small town southwest of Lake Pontchartrain in the northern outskirts of New Orleans. The folks who lived in Frenier Beach and the surrounding hamlets tended to be blue-collar people, German immigrants who made a living farming or logging. They had no roads, no electricity, and no doctors, which is maybe why they turned to Aunt Julia for her spiritual intercessions, despite her eccentricities.

But Aunt Julia's health started to decline in 1915, and supposedly, her mind went (further), too. She passed away on September 29, 1915, purportedly mumbling her song as she drifted away from this earth: "One day I'm gonna die, and I'm gonna take you all with me." And then, not six hours later, a category-3 storm hurtled through New Orleans, roaring through the levees and plucking cypress trees out of the earth by their roots. Buildings were uplifted and roads and rails were washed away. Oyster boats—and much of the economy—were sunk. In total, an estimated 300 people perished. The devastating hurricane wiped Frenier Beach and two neighboring towns clean off the map—just as Aunt Julia had sung.

DO IT

The best way to explore the Manchac Swamp's web of bayous and sloughs is by canoe or kayak. Put in at any of the launches off Old US 55 (30.162814, -90.444582 is a good one) and explore the channels north and east, based on water levels and access. Stay in the marshlands between Lakes Maurepas and Pontchartrain and keep your eyes peeled for Aunt Julia's ghost, who's been spotted cackling at the edge of the water. Experienced navigators only; practice gator safety. A number of outfitters in the area also offer guided tours.

Blackbeard

Ocracoke Island, Hammock Hills Nature Trail,
Cape Hatteras National Seashore, North Carolina

W E LIKE to think of pirates more as characters than a real part of our history. A pirate is something fun to dress up as and, when you're a kid, to aspire to become. But, that's kind of like romanticizing terrorists, rapists, and slave-traders. This is not the sort of recap that would earn you an A+ in any history courses, but the really basic timeline of piracy in North America goes like this: In the early 1700s, cross-Atlantic trade began to boom. Meanwhile, the War of the Spanish Succession ended in 1715, leaving thousands of military-trained sailors without work—and you know what they say about idle hands. At the time, it's estimated that more than 2,000 pirates were terrorizing the Caribbean and the eastern seaboard of the States. The Royal Crown was simply overmatched, so, in a last-ditch effort to quell the seas, the naval officers conspired to, at the very least, bring down Blackbeard.

Widely considered the face of piracy at the time (and even today), Blackbeard was a ruthless man. He subsisted mostly on intimidation—he'd ignite fuses in the tangled tendrils of his full-bodied beard before battle—but had no reservations about using brute force. In one tale, he even murdered his first mate in front of his crew so the latter "wouldn't forget who he was." In another, he blockaded Charleston, South Carolina, plundering at least five ships, and held several prominent citizens hostage until city officials gave him costly medical supplies on the house. In just two years at sea, Blackbeard captured more than thirty ships.

Between adventures, Blackbeard would return to present-day North Carolina's Outer Banks. He made a life there with at least one of his fourteen wives, where he could maintain a low profile amid the scads of barrier islands. Plus, the governor at the time, a man by the name of Charles Eden, was himself corrupt. In return for some of Blackbeard's spoils, Eden pardoned the pirate on at least two occasions.

So when Lt. Robert Maynard led two sloops with Union Jacks snapping in the wind into Bath, North Carolina, for the sole purpose of killing Blackbeard, it was likely a sight to behold. A parade of sorts, the ships sailed into the Outer Banks and ultimately cornered Blackbeard between the mainland and Ocracoke Island in the Pamlico Sound. Blackbeard and his crew were vastly outnumbered, but put up a fight that would inspire moviemakers today. When Maynard inspected Blackbeard's corpse, he would note in his logbook that the man suffered five gunshots and twenty sword slashes before he finally passed.

But recall that this battle was about cleaning up the seas and bringing down the face of piracy. So, perhaps taking his charge too literally, Maynard decapitated the dead pirate and lashed his head, big black beard and all, to the bowsprit of his ship, a sort of trophy or ornament to proudly display on his voyage back to Virginia. After, Maynard heaved the headless body overboard, and, legend has it, the corpse swam three laps around the naval ship before disappearing in Davy Jones's Locker.

DO IT

Visitors to both Hatteras and Ocracoke Islands have reported seeing "Teach's Light," believed to be the ghost of Blackbeard (real name: Edward Teach) swimming beneath the surface in search of his head, near the inland shores. But, for the sake of accuracy, your best bet is probably Ocracoke, where the pirate actually met his demise. (According to one legend, Ocracoke was named when Blackbeard, impatient for the sun to rise, shouted, "Oh, crow, cock!") The only way to get to Ocracoke is by boat, so paddle or take a ferry (ncdot.gov/ferry), then make your way over to the Hammock Hills trailhead (35.125481, -75.923832) to try the 0.8-miler, which wends through maritime woods and dunes to the salt marsh overlooking the Pamlico Sound. Paddlers can kayak through the Pamlico to the exact spot where Blackbeard supposedly still looks for his head: Launch from Ocracoke and follow the shore southwest to the inlet before Portsmouth.

The Hurricane Haint

Hurricane Creek, Cub Branch Trail, Big South Fork National River & Recreation Area, Tennessee

"HEY, GUYS, I think I see something!"
"Shut up and go to bed!"
"No, I'm serious! Give me your camera!"

It was midnight on a summer evening in 1986 and four teenage boys were camping near the confluence of the Big South Fork of the Cumberland River and Hurricane Creek in northern Tennessee, near the Kentucky state line. It's beautiful country—a remote corner of the Cumberland Plateau defined by lush gorges, sandstone bluffs, and the free-flowing Big South Fork—but that's not why the boys were there. It was a dare.

The area used to be inhabited by coal miners and loggers. You can still see evidence of their old homesteads, farms, and cemeteries, and there are dilapidated roads that seemingly lead to nowhere—if you know where to look. The deep hollows are at once arresting, but also creepy, deep black holes carved into the rock with no end in sight. It's no wonder locals began spinning rumors of a ghost living in the Big South Fork's recesses. In the South, they call spirits like that boogers or haints, and this particular one was dubbed the Hurricane Haint. Its origin is unclear, but that's how rumors are.

The four friends pitched their tent on the sandbar at the mouth of Hurricane Creek, just east of the Big South Fork. They were horsing around and tossing sticks and rocks into the water where the two rivers met. The objects would spin around in the eddies and disappear—a logical corollary for a whirlpool, but at night in a supposed haunted area, the mind plays tricks. The boys considered that perhaps the Haint was at work, snatching their sticks and rocks. They were tense, trying to prove their bravery to each other, and after sunset, they began throwing firecrackers into their campfire and spooking one another with made-up stories of the Hurricane Haint, one later told the *Knoxville News Sentinel*.

By midnight, three of the boys opted to go to bed, while one stayed out, huddled by the campfire. Whether he was assigned the post of lookout or he was simply too wired to consider sleeping is unknown, but shortly after his friends retired, he spied, clearly, a ball of light hovering overhead some ten feet from the tent. Reluctantly, one of the boys stuck his camera out the nylon door. The one outside grabbed it and feverishly snapped three photos with the flash.

And that was that. Several months allegedly passed before the boy who owned the camera even thought to develop the film. But when he did, he discovered the results of the three shots: two completely black and indecipherable pictures and one of a grove of trees with a glowing mass hovering amid the branches. The latter has since been published (Google "hurricane haint") and ultimately became the focal point of any discussion about the so-called Haint. Photography professionals have apparently vouched for it, suggesting that it in no way was Photoshopped, nor the product of a faulty development process.

So does the Haint actually exist? Is it hiding in a dark hollow behind a bend in the Big South Fork? Is it the spirit of an old miner or logger or someone who drowned? Or is it just a figment of a rumor that's taken hold among the old oaks and hickories of the Cumberland Plateau, escalating in scope by way of an inexplicable photo? We dare you to go set up a tent and see for yourself.

DO IT

Find the Cub Branch Trail at the end of Cliff Terry Road (36.588730, -84.569596). The path heads west toward the Big South Fork before ultimately bending north into Kentucky to the Slavens Branch trailhead. Do it end to end in an 8.2-mile shuttle hike (leave a second car at 36.617355, -84.544169), or do it as an out-and-back: Hike about 4.2 miles west to the confluence of the Big South Fork and Hurricane Creek before tracing your steps to the trailhead.

The Underworld

Tallulah Falls, Gorge Floor Trail, Tallulah Gorge State Park, Georgia

THERE'S A love story that's told around this part of the country. The details change version to version, but the gist is the same: There's a strapping, young Cherokee warrior who falls for a beautiful maiden with cascading locks of black hair. He proves his devotion to the girl by fasting for seven days, and then she relents and agrees to wed. It's a normal enough story to this point. But then the damsel proclaims, "If you tell anyone where we go or what you see, you will surely die."

He happily agrees and the two set out to travel to her home, where they plan to wed. They cross streams, zigzag through the sun-dappled poplar and oak woods, and arrive at the Tallulah River. There, she ushers him into her home, a grotto beneath Tallulah Falls. But the listener—or, in this case, reader—must understand that Tallulah Falls is no romantic setting.

Hidden in the fringes of the southern Appalachians, Tallulah Gorge is a 2-mile-long gash in the earth's crust, like Georgia is splitting at the seams from the inside out. Its namesake river, a torrent of white-water, surges between its near-vertical, 1,000-foot-tall rock walls. In one mile-long stretch, it crashes more than 500 feet down half a dozen rock shelves—Tallulah Falls. The cascade is so violent that centuries-old Cherokee tales suggest thunder originated there.

So the Cherokee warrior hesitates, suddenly skeptical of his betrothed. He's at the threshold of the cave, the Tallulah River coursing overhead, when the woman removes her hair, revealing a head that's "as smooth as a pumpkin."[7] She asks him to sit down beside her, but the man—now "more frightened than ever"—sees only an angry turtle where a chair should have been. A thunderstorm commences, and the woman offers him a bracelet. The warrior looks up to see the woman beginning to string a live snake around his wrist. It's chaos.

When the warrior comes to, he's alone in the forest with no trace of the grotto or his fiancée. He hurries back to his settlement, where he discovers that he's been missing so long that he's been left for dead. He explains where he's been to his fellow tribespeople, "but in seven days he died, for no one can come back from the underworld and tell it and live."

Consider that a fair warning. Visitors have reported seeing an amorphous Cherokee warrior as early as 1891, calling it the Ghost of Tallulah Falls, while hikers today still report strange noises echoing from behind the falls. Some say they feel odd sensations on the gorge floor. But no one is too specific—for obvious reasons.

DO IT

For the best tour of Tallulah Gorge, nab a permit to hike to the canyon floor. From the trailhead (34.739807, -83.390609), link up with the Hurricane Falls Trail and take it to the bottom of the chasm (note: the park claims roughly 600 metal steps, so you should be reasonably fit). There pick up the Gorge Floor Trail, which follows the river a little more than a mile downstream past a handful of cascades, which, together, make up Tallulah Falls. Retrace your steps on the return.

Mid-Atlantic

A Breath of Fresh Air

Mammoth Cave, Guided Tour, Mammoth Cave National Park, Kentucky

WHEN SCIENTISTS removed thirty-year-old timber from an old mine in Mammoth Cave only to discover that the planks had not yet even begun to rot, at least one man was paying attention. Curious, Dr. John Croghan began monitoring local journals and accounts from the area and saw a pattern. Dead bats showed no signs of decay. Centuries-old human corpses, even, remained perfectly intact.

Convinced the air in Mammoth Cave held inexplicable healing powers, Dr. Croghan purchased the hollow outright, slaves included, for $10,000 in 1839. Within the next few years, the doctor orchestrated a subterranean sanitarium. Sixteen tuberculosis patients lived among crude huts, marinating in the cave's constant air temperature of 54 degrees Fahrenheit. They reported improved health, inspiring the doctor to draw up plans for a massive underground hotel, which guests were bound to visit when news of the cave's magical air spread across the country.

And, yet, maybe sanitarium isn't even the oddest application in Mammoth Cave's history. Some 4,000 years ago, early Native Americans are said to have used the sunken labyrinth as a sacred burial ground, giving dead bodies a natural passage back to the earth. After that, white settlers repurposed the cave into a saltpeter mine. They used an army of slaves to mine the cave's innards for the crystalline salt and then sold it in batches to mineral companies like DuPont, which used it to manufacture gunpowder during the War of 1812. After the war, Mammoth Cave was privately owned for local tourism, until Croghan stepped into the scene.

By the 1840s, tourists visiting Mammoth Cave would pass through the sanitarium to gawk at the ghostly figures who stumbled weakly along the paths between huts in floor-length dressing gowns, their hacking and coughing reverberating through the dark chambers. Despite their and Dr. Croghan's optimism, however, the patients weren't healed. The dank air actually ravaged their lungs, ultimately killing five. The surviving patients were brought up to the surface, where they succumbed to consumption the normal way—above ground. In 1849, Dr. Croghan himself died of the disease.

After the failed sanitarium experiment, Mammoth Cave continued to exchange hands and adopt new uses. Some normal, like a roadside attraction, where guests could explore its snakelike passageways. Others not so much, like a public viewing area where guests could see the corpse of a man who'd perished in its depths displayed in a glass-topped coffin. But for the largest-known cave network in the world (boasting more than 400 miles of explored subterranean passageways), perhaps national park is its best identity. In 1941, more than ninety years after Dr. Croghan passed, Mammoth Cave was designated and protected. Now, hikers can explore its bowels on guided tours, and, though you won't see any tuberculosis patients, you may hear them coughing.

DO IT

Tours of Mammoth Cave change year to year, but make sure you sign up for one that is slated to pass the "Tuberculosis Huts." In the past, good options have been the 3-mile Violet City Lantern Tour (you carry kerosene lanterns like tourists did 150 years ago) and the 1-mile Gothic Avenue Tour. Prices vary and tours generally require a reservation. After, knock out the 0.5-mile Heritage Trail from the Mammoth Cave Hotel (37.186190, -86.101184), which wends (above ground) past the Old Guides Cemetery, where the tuberculosis patients are buried.

Gimme Shelter

Punchbowl Shelter, Appalachian Trail, George Washington National Forest, Virginia

THERE ARE dozens of "Bluff Mountains" in the United States. There are at least four in Virginia alone. And yet, perhaps the least impressive Bluff Mountain—one that barely surpasses 3,000 feet in elevation and doesn't even register on some topo maps—displays a summit plaque. The bronze-plated stone honors Ottie Cline Powell, the youngest person to have scaled Bluff's spruce-covered slopes at the time. Ottie was just four years old when he summited. But it was a mistake—a fatal one.

Ottie lived with his parents and seven brothers and sisters in Amherst County, just east of the Blue Ridge foothills. On November 9, 1891, the blue-eyed, sandy-haired boy walked to the schoolhouse with the other children like he always did. It was chilly, the aftermath of the season's first snowstorm, and Ottie's teacher had burned through the firewood supply. She sent her students out of the classroom to harvest more, but Ottie never returned.

A community-wide search failed to return him before night fell and temperatures dropped even more. As news of Ottie's disappearance spread, the search purportedly grew to 1,000 people strong—and still no Ottie. He had vanished.

It wasn't until the following spring, nearly 5 months later, when a hunting dog tracked Ottie's scent to the top of Bluff Mountain, 7 miles from the schoolhouse and more than 2,000 feet above. Details get fuzzy thereon, but some versions say that his remains were found with undigested chestnuts, an indication that perhaps Ottie didn't suffer long.

Whatever the fate of his earthly body, however, Ottie's spirit is still restless. Despite the Appalachian creed of trail magic (which inspires thru-hikers to decorate Ottie's memorial with toy cars and other small trinkets) Ottie has been heard shouting for help along the stretch of trail north of Bluff. Worse, he torments hikers who are posting up in the Punchbowl Shelter, a three-sided lean-to just north of the mountain off the AT. Hiker reports in the shelter's logbook describe a ghost that prods sleeping guests in the ribs, messes with their belongings, and laments that he can't find his parents.

One entry details a thru-hiker's particularly vivid memory of encountering Ottie's sobbing ghost in the Punchbowl Shelter. He says he awoke in the middle of the night and very clearly saw Ottie's ghost huddled in a corner of the lean-to, crying. "You might think I dreamed this," he goes on, "...but when I woke this morning, the clothes in my pack had been taken out and folded into little squares. Also, there was a small pile of dried-out chestnuts on them."

DO IT

To tag Bluff Mountain and the Punchbowl Shelter in one go, your best bet is to pick up the Appalachian Trail in Snowden. Find the trailhead near the intersection of VA 130 and VA 812 (37.597137, -79.389507), then take the AT nearly 11 miles north, covering some 2,700 feet of elevation, to the Punchbowl lean-to (crest 3,372-foot Bluff Mountain near mile 9.5). Spend the night in the first-come, first-served shelter, then either retrace your steps or arrange a shuttle and continue roughly 0.5 mile to the Blue Ridge Parkway (37.676325, -79.333727).

Bloody Lane

The Sunken Road, Bloody Lane Trail, Antietam National Battlefield, Maryland

"THEY WERE singing," a young schoolboy feverishly wrote in his journal. The boy was describing the reenactment he and a few of his classmates had seen that day as a homework assignment following up their visit to Antietam National Battlefield, a relatively new national park. But there was something odd about his recollection. In fact, there had been no reenactment that day.

The boy and his classmates were learning about the Battle of Antietam on the day of the field trip. Perhaps only Civil War buffs recall the massacre's importance, but it ultimately begat the Emancipation Proclamation. The country's single bloodiest day—an estimated 131,000 troops were engaged, resulting in more than 22,000 casualties—quickly became a stark contrast with the beauty of where soldiers were battling. Swaths of little bluestem grasses and farmlands are hemmed in by stands of sycamores, while the Antietam Creek, a tributary of the Potomac, lazily snakes through the picture. The scene is so charmingly simple, it looks like a child's drawing. And yet, on September 17, 1862, Sharpsburg, Maryland, would be tarnished forever.

At dawn, Maj. Gen. Joseph Hooker and his Union corps mounted an assault on Robert E. Lee's flank. Attacks—and counterattacks—ensued, but, despite the Union's strength (nearly twice as many men), the Confederates held their ground. Toward late morning, Confederate major general Daniel Harvey Hill led his division of 2,600 men to the top of a low ridge that spanned the field. A dirt lane, which had been worn down over the years by rain and farmers' wagons, followed the ridgeline, like a trench. It was an obviously strategic defensive position, so Hill ordered his men into the sunken road, where they would wait for Union advances.

When Union major general William H. French and his 5,500 men approached the natural trench, the Confederates swarmed out of the sunken road, firing at a range of less than 100 yards. Men of both sides fought for more than three hours in what would become the bloodiest one-day battle in American military history. Soldiers "lay as thick as autumn leaves along a narrow lane cut below the natural surface, into which they seemed to have tumbled," Union general Alpheus S. Williams later wrote. The sunken road would become known as Bloody Lane.

It was the centerpiece of the schoolboy's field trip, as it tends to be for any visitor. People report feeling very introspective when they visit, which isn't entirely surprising. But what is surprising, is that people have noted hearing drumbeats, chanting, flags snapping in the wind, and gunfire. Some have noted odors of gunpowder. Sometimes, people even report reenactments when none have happened.

DO IT

Follow the footsteps of Union soldiers as they pursued the Confederates in the sunken road on the 1.6-mile Bloody Lane Trail. From the visitor center (39.474233, -77.744623), head out on the Bloody Lane Trail and follow the loop clockwise past Mumma and Roulette Farms to the natural trench and back to the trailhead. Check the website ahead of time for a schedule of events—in case what you're seeing isn't actually a reenactment.

No Dignity in Death

Letchworth Village Cemetery, Long Path, Cheesecote Mountain Town Park, New York

ETWEEN THE birch woods, mossy hollows, and periodic long-range views, there are enough highlights on the 350-plus-mile Long Path to refuel any nature-starved New Yorker. But if you don't look closely enough, you might miss one of the best—or worst, depending on your stance. Before Catskill Park, before the Shawangunk Mountains, and before Harriman State Park, the Long Path threads through Cheesecote Mountain Town Park, a tiny slice of metro-wilderness. There, the trail ducks beneath a hardwood canopy and past a haunted cemetery. But if you don't know where to look, you'll miss the latter. There is no signage to mark its existence, not even a collection of tombstones. Rows of metal Ts poke out of the clay, looking more like a vegetable garden than a graveyard. But it's not all that surprising that people who earned no respect in life would garner the same treatment in death.

Beneath the earth in this random trailside glade lie the corpses of more than 800 people who were sentenced to a life at Letchworth Village, a "state institution for the segregation of the epileptic and feeble-minded." The facility first opened its doors in Thiells, New York, in 1911 as a supposedly more progressive solution for developmentally disabled people than, say, an asylum. The idea was ripe: A self-sustaining, self-contained village for patients and attendants certainly seemed more productive than sentencing people to an almshouse. But things devolved over time.

At the onset, well before political correctness was a consideration, patients were divided into one of three categories of "feeble-mindedness." They were, from worst to less worse: "idiot," "imbecile," and "moron." Based on their intelligence categories, patients would be assigned a job or task, like farming, cooking, sewing, cleaning, or welding. It was a radical departure from the day's prescribed treatment for developmental issues, and, if you can get past the cringeworthy diagnoses, maybe even a good idea—in theory.

But reports from the 1930s quickly revealed that, in practice, it wasn't working. Letchworth Village housed 3,000 patients by the mid-1930s, and the place was simply overcrowded and underfunded. An exposé in the 1940s revealed that the treatment itself was "neglectful." Photographs were published of patients unwashed and naked and sleeping on the floor. In 1950, the first trial case of the polio vaccine was tested on Letchworth Village children. It's probably worth noting that the vaccine would ultimately be developed into the one we use today (and none of the 20 children experienced adverse reactions), but that's how expendable Letchworth Village patients were viewed to be. They were lab rats.

People eventually realized that normalization and inclusion in everyday society is a much better treatment for people with developmental disabilities than segregation, but not before erecting the 2-acre Letchworth Village Cemetery. In lieu of names, the grave markers are numbered to grant family members of the deceased full anonymity from their "defective" relatives. If it makes you squirm, you're not alone: Long Path hikers have reported hearing crying and whimpering echoing from the cemetery as they walk past. Some have even caught glimpses of people in medical gowns wandering among the graves, but the amorphous figures don't show up in photographs—which is probably how their relatives would have wanted it.

DO IT

Park in the Mt. Ivy Park & Ride lot (41.186042, -74.037626) and find a worn footpath on the west side of Palisades Interstate Parkway via the underpass. Take it north into Cheesecote Mountain Town Park, where you'll meet the Long Path near Cheesecote Pond at mile 2.5. Reach the Letchworth Village Cemetery near mile 3.4. Letchworth Village officially closed its doors in 1996, but you can wander amid the neoclassical buildings nearby (don't enter). From the cemetery, either retrace your steps for a 6.8-mile out-and-back, or continue about 6 miles to the Lake Skannatati parking area (41.2420145, -74.1023301), where you should leave a shuttle car if you wish to make it a 9.4-mile point-to-point trek.

The Devil Child

Pine Barrens, Macri Trail, Wells Mills County Park, New Jersey

"MAY THE Devil take this one!" Jane Leeds cried, giving birth to both her thirteenth child and the greatest legend in New Jersey lore.

Leeds lived in the Pine Barrens, a 1.1-million-acre tract of gloomy pine woods and swamps that stretches across the coastal plain in southern New Jersey. While stunted conifers grow without issue in the area, the region is so named because barely anything else does: The soil is too dusty and acidic—called "sugar sand"—to support crops. In fact, the only other plants that seem to thrive in the boggy Pine Barrens are carnivorous, like pitcher plants, sundews, and bladderworts. It's the sort of place you imagine gave rise to George Lucas's planet Dagobah or *The Princess Bride*'s treacherous Fire Swamp.

But in actuality, it was the setting of Leeds's humble home in the 1700s. Like the other people who lived there at the time—derogatorily called "pineys"—Leeds was poor and struggling to make ends meet. Since she couldn't escape her poverty, the story goes, she angrily cursed her thirteenth child.

After, she didn't bear a normal infant. Disfigured and mutilated, it was less a child than a monster. It bore an elongated horse's head, and its face resembled that of a collie. It had cloven hooves and a serpentlike body covered in scales. Immediately, the grotesque child grew before Leeds's eyes until it was more than 20 feet long, slithering and clambering around the ramshackle cabin until it found an escape through the chimney. The monster darted into the Pinelands, never to be seen again—until the latter half of the century.

Locals began reporting that something was terrorizing their farm-steads. In some cases, they'd find piles of livestock remains, and in other cases the animals went missing altogether. Many of the region's cows stopped producing milk, and the fish that were once abundant in the freshwater streams began to disappear. Hunters tried to trap the beast, ministers tried to exorcise it, and military men tried to destroy it. But no one could. The ones who spotted it cited its massive, leathery wings, and many noticed unusually large, unidentifiable hoofprints in the soft soil. Children started going missing.

Sightings continued into the 1900s, and still no one could catch or kill the creature. Notably, a reputable postmaster from Bristol, Pennsylvania, claimed to have seen it, describing it as a mammoth and glowing crane with a high-pitched whistle. A Pinelands couple with no history of fibbing claimed to have seen a winged horse spewing fire and walking on its hind legs across the roof of their shed. Other townspeople claimed to have seen it, noting its massive fangs or its huge gait or its kangaroo-like hind legs. Rewards were offered to anyone who could trap it, dead or alive.

And by 1993, the beast was still on the loose. A forest ranger named John Irwin was patrolling the Mullica River when he stumbled across a monster some 6 feet tall with horns and matted black fur. Irwin's description didn't seem to match that from the original legend, or any of the other accounts from the centuries between, but perhaps it's more comforting to think that the Jersey Devil is some kind of shapeshifter. The alternative is, of course, that there is a slew—literally dozens—of different monsters wreaking havoc in the Pine Barrens.

DO IT

Search for the Jersey Devil on the 8.4-mile Macri Trail in Wells Mills County Park. From the parking lot (39.795266, -74.276247), cir-cle through the pines and wetlands, keeping an eye out for wings, claws, scales, hooves, or anything unusual. The 53.5-mile, pink-blazed Batona Trail is a good option for people with more time; the route traverses the Pinelands from unincorporated Ong's Hat through Bass River State Forest.

The Woman in the Mist

Glen Onoko Falls, Glen Onoko Loop, Lehigh Gorge State Park, Pennsylvania

"GLEN ONOKO Falls" seems almost a misnomer when you catch a glimpse of the thing. More of a catchall phrase, Glen Onoko Falls describes a 0.6-mile-long section of Glen Onoko Run, a free-flowing trough of whitewater that careens some 800 feet down a narrow valley to the surging Lehigh. It plunges over a number of rock shelves, the tallest drop of which is more than 60 feet. It's a stunner, in all senses of the word, and the obvious centerpiece of a trail that was constructed sometime around the turn of the twentieth century.

That trail was the handiwork of tycoons who established the Hotel Wahnetah in the late 1800s. Named in homage to the local Native American tribe, the Victorian-styled resort was accessed by two rails that would deliver urbanites from the steaming, crowded cities to the lush, undeveloped Lehigh Gorge. The lodge boasted luxuries for the time, like a dance pavilion, tennis courts, an 80-foot-long bar, and a trail network that included the route to the whitewater torrent.

Employees at the lodge soon started calling the cascade "Glen Onoko Falls" after a Wahnetah princess who met her demise in its rocky depths. Supposedly, Onoko fell in love with a white man, whom she was not permitted to marry. When word reached her that her tribe planned to execute the man, she threw herself over the precipice and into the waterfall that now bears her name. The pink rhododendrons that grow alongside the run were said to be stained by her blood—and Hotel Wahnetah officials had no shame in using the story to drum up local tourism.

They constructed a trail to a vantage of the plunging water and promoted it heavily. But whereas today trail-building is an actual science of switchback angles, erosion patterns, and ecology principles, in the late 1800s the trails from Hotel Wahnetah were probably more like paths of least resistance. The trail from the lodge to the waterfall, for instance, was a straight shot over rocky outcroppings, across moss-covered boulders, and through the underbrush.

Unfortunately, a series of wildfires tore through the Lehigh Gorge in the 1910s, shutting down Hotel Wahnetah for good and effectively putting an end to the area's resort era. But the trail to Glen Onoko Falls survived, and, in fact, more than a century later, is the basis for the one we continue to use today. But, as it was in the late 1800s, it's still heady: The new trail ascends some 800 feet from the base of the gorge, paralleling the run and requiring class-3 climbing moves in spots. The spray from the waterfall can make it slippery, and slick moss can make it near-impossible to gain foot purchase. While it may have, at one time, sported wooden handholds or railings, those have since burned down or otherwise deteriorated because the trail is exposed and largely unprotected.

It's unsurprising that as many as a dozen hikers have fallen to their deaths on this relatively unknown path—but what is surprising, is that on clear days the ghost of a young Native American woman is believed to appear in the mist at the base of the biggest drop every morning at 9:15 a.m. She's veiled, as a bride, and solemn—either because she lost her love or because so many others mirrored her fate.

DO IT

Find the trailhead north of a U-bend in the Lehigh River (40.883405, -75.760263) and head north on the Glen Onoko Loop. It's about 2 miles if you don't take any of the spurs, but plan to linger. If you do it clockwise, pass the tiered Glen Onoko Falls on the first leg (as well as the misty splash zone where Onoko's ghost has been spotted). There are three main shelves, and footing can be sketchy. Hikers have reported stumbling across old ruins of the Hotel Wahnetah near the top. Loop back through the forest for an easier downclimb.

Dirty Money

South Mountain, Appalachian Trail, South Mountain State Park, Maryland

NOT MUCH is known about Daniel Wise. He had two children, was probably poor, and, for some reason, never fought in the Civil War. Instead, he tended a farm near Fox's Gap, a low valley between two mounds of Maryland's South Mountain. If he was trying to evade the war, his luck turned on September 14, 1862, when the Battle of South Mountain pitted more than 50,000 troops atop the northernmost ridge of the Blue Mountains. They funneled into Fox's Gap, charging through Wise's fields and advancing through Maryland.

At the end of the day, Wise's farmland, stained red with blood, must have been unrecognizable. Body parts littered the grass and corpses lay thick across the valley. Smoke hung low, clouding the scene. It was a Union victory, though it must not have felt like it at the time. Wise, it's said, converted his farmhouse into an infirmary and helped the remaining soldiers, battered and bloodied as they were, comb his fields for survivors. After, the men set out to bury the dead, but there were so many that, legend has it, the Union men had to move on before the work was finished. Offering Wise $5 per body he buried, the soldiers left.

Wise seemed an honest man—trying to make an honest living—and dutifully set out to do as he was commissioned. But digging a 6-foot-long trench would seem an arduous task even in the best circumstances, if any existed. And these were not ideal conditions; the dirt in Fox's Gap was less soil than it was clay, and it was choked with rocks. In two days' time, Wise had buried only a few men, and the odor of the deceased was suffocating him. And so, Daniel Wise heaved fifty-eight soldiers into his well.

HAUNTED HIKES

If anyone deserves a proper burial, it's certainly a soldier. And the crop of men that lay in a heap in Wise's well themselves seemed to not have appreciated their unceremonious treatment; they haunted Wise for a dozen years before they were finally reinterred in the Washington Confederate Cemetery in Hagerstown. Wise may have been let off the hook afterward, but Appalachian Trail thru-hikers today still claim to hear the thuds of falling bodies into the well when they pass through Fox's Gap.

DO IT

You can thru-hike the Maryland section of the Appalachian Trail in a hefty weekend if you're feeling frisky; it's about 40.5 miles end to end. You'll cruise up to Fox's Gap near mile 16.5 of a northbound hike (24 of a southbounder). If you're looking for something shorter, traverse South Mountain on a 14.4-mile point-to-point: From the Appalachian trailhead on Reno Mountain Road (39.470546, -77.617615), hike north through Fox's Gap and along the spine of South Mountain to a small parking area on MD 17 (39.630001, -77.558937). There are a few roads that bisect this trip if you want to make it even shorter.

Theories Abound

Lums Pond, Swamp Forest Trail, Lums Pond State Park, Delaware

THE BLOOD-CURDLING screams heard at night in this state park are a stark contrast to its appearance. In fact, the spectrum of beauty that the seasons bring to Lums Pond is truly a spectacle any hiker would be lucky to behold. Even in winter, supposedly the ugliest time of year, Lums Pond is so peaceful, it looks like an old-timey, black-and-white photo: the barren trees tickled with frost, the slate-colored lake still as a pane of glass.

When spring rolls around, brilliant green buds begin popping like kernels of corn and the pond gets new life—literally—as it adopts its old shade of jade. By the time summer hits, the hardwoods are cloaked in an impossibly bright shade of green. But locals know the best is yet to come, because with fall's arrival, the sweet gums transform red and purple, the black cherries orange, and the maples the sort of crimson only an East Coaster can appreciate. Lums Pond basks in its new frame, often reflecting the color, so in a picture you can't tell which way is up and which way is down.

But when night falls, that serenity seems to disappear. Campers report hearing desperate screams from a female and sometimes even pleas—but they're fleeting, the sort of noise you think you've heard, but then aren't quite sure. Some people suggest that there was a kidnapping nearby, and the young girl was brutally murdered at the banks of Lums Pond. Others have offered a "lover's leap" sort of legend about a heartbroken woman who intentionally drowned herself. Still others have drawn a connection to the Underground Railroad, one route of which is believed to have run through this area. On its website, the state of Delaware propounds that a runaway girl in the 1870s was "taken into the woods" and killed. "The murderer was never apprehended," the web page concludes.

There are a lot of theories floating around, but really only the ghost herself knows the answer. Until she reveals her fate, it's best to simply take solace in the beauty of Lums Pond—during the day, of course.

DO IT

Lums Pond State Park is closed to hiking every day at sunset, for obvious reasons. To experience it at night, you'll need to book one of the equestrian campgrounds (destateparks.com). During the day, do your reconnaissance on the Swamp Forest Trail: From the parking lot (39.561374, -75.720443), loop around the pond on an easy, 6.4-mile circuit.

Smoke on the Water

Sandstone Falls, New River, New River Gorge National River, West Virginia

HEN THE water was low or the weather was dry, you could bet that old Samuel Richmond's gristmill would still be spinning. Even when a wretched drought hit the Northeast in the mid-1800s, business was booming for Richmond. He lived at the base of Sandstone Falls on the banks of the New River, where the torrent, spanning some 1,500 feet across, bores through the Appalachian Plateau. There may not have been a better spot for a mill, and Richmond was, as they say, rolling in it.

Richmond was a kind man who treated his employees well. He'd often work alongside them and, at the end of the day, he'd ferry them back across the New River if they lived on the other side. He was stubborn in his old age, and was, in fact, too old to serve in the war, but that didn't mean he didn't foster any opinions on the matter. Old texts point out that, not only was he a staunch Union man, but, in his stubbornness, Richmond had engendered extreme bitterness toward the South. People said it was the one topic that'd really ruffle the old man's feathers and turn his mood sour.

One day in 1863, in what would become almost the perfect middle of the four-year Civil War, Richmond grabbed his hat and coat and set out to paddle his good employee, Allen Vincent, back across the river. As he headed out the front door, his wife urged him not to go. She didn't know why, but she was sure something bad would come of it. But night was falling and Richmond didn't want his friend to be stuck on the Raleigh side until daybreak, so he shook his wife's unease aside and walked the half of a mile or so south down the banks to his canoe and hopped in. He ushered

Vincent in, and the two pushed off and headed out into the New River, the bow slicing through the calm waters and made their way toward the folds of green slopes on the Summers side.

The two docked safely on the banks near Laurel Creek, and Richmond bid his friend farewell. He stuck an oar into the mud and pushed back out, gliding backward through the river toward home.

Richmond heard it before he felt it, and instinctively held his hand up to his chest, where the warm blood began to soak through his shirt and coat his fingers. He looked up to see two men scamper out from the underbrush across the way. Through sheer will, the old man managed to paddle back toward his homestead, where he collapsed in the shallow water. A few neighbors rushed to his aid and hauled his limp body inside, but he was already dead. He had been shot through the lungs by a man whose name is of no consequence; what is, is that this man was a Confederate sympathizer and supporter of secession.

The cascade near Richmond's homestead and gristmill, along with a handful of other landmarks and structures in the area, would be named in the old man's honor. They'd keep the Richmond tag for nearly a century before the type of rock at the local quarry began to take over as the area's namesake and identity. But, like his ever-running mill, the area still couldn't shake old Samuel Richmond. Locals continued to see a bobbing lantern float across the New River in the years that followed his death, as though the man were continuing to make his rounds, back and forth across the water. Even today, hikers and paddlers in the area report seeing the ghost light hovering above the surface on calm days around twilight, stubborn as ever.

DO IT

There's a short boardwalk that you can hike across for the best vantage of Sandstone (formerly Richmond's) Falls (find parking near 37.759214, -80.905535), but this area hosts some of the best kayaking in the area. To experience the New River by boat as Richmond himself did, try the 11-mile section from Bluestone Dam to Sandstone Falls. Put in near the confluence of the Bluestone and New Rivers (37.612401, -80.916626), then head downstream (north). Expect class-I to -III whitewater in normal conditions and flow. Sandstone Falls is a mandatory portage.

A Walk in the Woods

Moose River Plains Wild Forest, Lost Ponds Trail, Adirondack Park, New York

J ACK COLONEY signed the trailhead register at Cedar River on June 6, 2006. He scrawled his return date—eight days later—across the page, seemingly in a hurry. It's no wonder why: The forty-five-year-old Coloney was an amateur photographer—and the Moose River Plains tract of Adirondack Park loves the camera. In June, the hardwoods are piercingly emerald. The streams and ponds are so clear you can see straight to the bottom. Moose munch on grasses in the shallows, black bears lumber through the undergrowth, birds begin nesting amid all the greenery. It's a scene that could inspire a Disney film. So, with camera in tow, Coloney set out for eight days of wilderness solitude.

On Coloney's intended return date, an off-duty ranger passed by his campsite near the Lost Ponds trailhead. It looked perfectly intact—tent set up, cook system ready to go, camera logbook at the ready—but there was no sign of Coloney. The ranger notified his superiors, and on June 17, when there was still no sign of the photographer, one of the most exhaustive search-and-rescue missions in the area's history was launched. It lasted ten days and tallied more than 4,000 man hours by a team of more than fifty rangers, New York police, Sheriff's Department officials, and volunteers. It covered a 35-square-mile area in the Adirondacks, but no clue of Coloney's whereabouts was ever discovered.

The forests in this area of the Adirondacks, in particular, are unforgiving. The hardwoods are exceedingly dense, offering only sporadic long-range views, while the relative flatness of the terrain provides very few landmarks from which hikers can orient themselves. The trails themselves are often overgrown, requiring hikers to bushwhack, even if their itineraries are fully on-trail. On top of all of that, there's something about this tract of woods that makes compasses go haywire. Some people argue it's the iron content in the soil, others suggest something deeper, but handheld compasses have been known to lose north, and the electronic compasses in cars simply stop working. It's almost like the forest wants you to lose your way.

The area is the site of some eighty individual search-and-rescue missions every year. So, really, it's miraculous that only seventeen hikers have gone missing—never to return—since the 1950s. Of those, seven disappeared outright, including Coloney, as though the forest ate them alive with no warning and no clues.

DO IT

The 1.2-mile Lost Ponds Trail begins off of Moose River Road (near 43.682059, -74.666798). Fittingly, the trail network around here doesn't appear on most USGS topos, so you'll want to find a map specific to the Moose River Plains (and maybe a knowledgeable buddy) before heading out. There are tent sites at the Lost Ponds. Note: There are at least a dozen "Lost Ponds" in New York alone and a "Lost Pond Trail" within 6 miles of this "Lost Ponds Trail." Don't become a victim of the Moose River Plains Wild Forest.

Hallowed Ground

Devil's Den, Billy Yank Trail, Gettysburg National Military Park, Pennsylvania

O N A COOL, foggy morning, a woman peered out over the battlefields of Gettysburg. She stood atop Little Round Top, a scalped hillock in the southern reaches of Gettysburg National Military Park, and sighed deeply as introspection overtook her. At that moment, she was fulfilling Lincoln's command in honoring "the brave men, living and dead, who struggled here." She hoisted a camera to her eye and panned across the rocky fields, but stopped suddenly. A shiver coursed through her body, and the hair on the back of her neck and arms prickled. She sensed that she was being watched, and spun around to see a man with shoulder-length hair, sullied clothing, bare feet, and a floppy, brimmed hat staring at her.

"What you're looking for is over there," he drawled in a thick southern accent. The woman followed his gaze to the west toward Devil's Den, a boulder-strewn valley below. But when she turned back around, the man was gone. He had vanished. The woman described the ragged man to park rangers, who purportedly were surprised; there was no reenactment on this particular day, so why was a man wandering the park in period garb? Weirder still, subsequent visitors began reporting encounters with a man of the same description. And, as in the first case, he never stuck around, often disappearing just as suddenly as he had appeared.

But the Hippie, as the ghostly Confederate soldier was later named, wasn't the only spirit supposedly lurking around Gettysburg. People later claimed to see a Union soldier marching around Little Round Top, posing and answering questions—yet he'd never appeared in any developed photographs. Other visitors reported malfunctioning cameras, while still

others said they heard the sounds of marching soldiers, galloping horses, cannon fire, and shouting when no reenactments were going on.

Scientists who study the paranormal agree that many spirits tend to hang around the sites of their deaths, so perhaps it's unsurprising that the bloodiest battle on American soil spawned so many ghost stories. Consider this: More than 7,000 men were killed during the four-day Battle of Gettysburg. More than 33,000 were gravely wounded. More than 10,000 were captured or missing in action. That's more than 51,000 casualties. When framed like that, maybe a few hundred ghost encounters aren't actually all that many.

DO IT

You can do Gettysburg as an auto tour, but then you'll miss out on the forests, meadows, and wetlands that make this park a worthy destination even without the history. Instead, tackle the 10-mile Billy Yank Trail from the Soldiers' National Cemetery (39.811074, -77.226205). Go clockwise, looping through cannon-flanked fields and past monuments and farms to crest Little Round Top near mile 3.7. From there, head west down to the granite maze of Devil's Den, where Confederate snipers hid and picked off so many Union soldiers that the creek supposedly ran red. Return to the main trail to climb Big Round Top for a view over the whole park, before circling back past monuments honoring Mississippi, Florida, and Virginia troops.

Tommyknockers

Maryland Mine, Gold Mine Trail, Chesapeake &
Ohio Canal National Historic Park, Maryland

"MR. INGALLS, I ain't doin' that job no more,"
declared the night watchman of the Maryland
Mine. The man had a lot of audacity giving up
on the gold mine, but he also had no shame: "A
ghost-looking man with eyes of fire and a tail
10 feet long crawled out of the shaft and disappeared in the forest," the
watchman continued.[8]

Tommyknockers are nothing new, but you'd be hard-pressed to get a
rugged, hypermasculine miner to express belief in the small, leprechaun-
like creatures. But not only did the watchman confess to having seen one,
so did a number of miners before him. By the time he left his post as
watchman, fear of tommyknockers was more like a full-fledged epidemic
and ultimately gained enough traction to aid in the Maryland Mine's
shuttering in 1908. The mine would reopen, only briefly, a few times in
the subsequent half-century when the price of gold rose enough to shake
the owner, but it would never be all that profitable and now exists only as
some boarded-up ruins.

Indeed, after the first shaft of the Maryland Mine was sunk near Great
Falls in 1867, it faced nothing but hardship. The gold was scant to begin
with—the miners would have to blast hunks of rock from the ground and
send them to mills to be crushed, so the ore could be siphoned from the
dust. As compared to other notable gold rushes of the country, Maryland's
was pitiful. And the prevalence of unnatural creatures certainly didn't help.

The stories of the tommyknockers really kicked off after a fateful
explosion in 1906. A handful of miners took a break in the hoist room, and

as legend has it, one set his candle-illuminated helmet on a table beside a stick of dynamite. The blast killed one man and launched the legend. Miners began reporting that their tools were misplaced, their lunches missing, and strange noises were echoing off the rock walls in the mine's deepest recesses. By the time work horses began refusing to go near the entrance, miners were quitting the job faster than they could be replaced.

When the watchman quit, publicizing the fear of tommyknockers in the area, the owner supposedly couldn't find anyone to take the job. People believed the mine was cursed. If that's true, then it remains so today: Legend has it that if you hear a tommyknocker, you're destined for tragedy yourself.

DO IT

You can still identify the old Maryland Mine's water tank, blacksmith shop, and parts of its original shafts from the 3.2-mile Gold Mine Trail. You can't enter the mine or any of its dilapidated structures, but listen closely for the footsteps of a tommyknocker beneath the surface when you reach the ruins (or don't, if you're superstitious). Pick up the loop from the Great Falls Tavern Visitor Center (39.000264, -77.248135).

In Cold Blood

Whiteoak Canyon, Appalachian Trail, Shenandoah National Park, Virginia

OLLIE WINANS felt alive in the woods. She loved good beer, cigarettes, and Phish, but the wilderness had her heart. So at twenty-four, she set out to become a guide, spending her days bagging peaks in Maine's Saddlebacks and canoeing through Minnesota's storied Boundary Waters. She wanted to start a service where she'd guide troubled women on outdoor expeditions, in the hopes that they'd experience the natural, life-changing power of the wilderness, like she did.

In two years' time, Winans found her counterpart in Julie Williams, a young woman who'd also experienced nature's gospel. Williams had studied geology in college, explored ancient civilizations abroad, and had somehow ended up on a women's adventure retreat in the liquid labyrinth of the Boundary Waters, where she met Winans. The two hit it off and set out to test their young relationship in Shenandoah, one of the country's finest national parks.

In May of 1996, the two were exploring gorges, glimpsing plunging waterfalls, and notching blufftop views over the Blue Ridge Mountains on a life-list trip through Shenandoah. They hiked sections of the Appalachian Trail's green tunnel, and, on night five, netted a particularly idyllic campsite on a bridle path just off the famous long path. It sat in a clearing amid old-growth hemlocks and beside a fern-lined stream. They were content. Maybe they lay in their tent and stared at the yellow nylon for a while before drifting off, or maybe sleep overtook the women quickly, but, despite how happy they were, their story ended that night.

When authorities located the yellow tent, they found Winans inside. Her wrists were bound, she was gagged, and her throat had been slit. She'd been dead nearly a week when they discovered her. Nearby, they found Williams in a heap, tangled with her sleeping bag. She had suffered the same gruesome fate.

There have been at least nine murders on the country's most-celebrated long path. In the large scheme of things, that statistic should actually be reassuring for hikers. You're thousands of times less likely to be the victim of a violent crime on the 2,189-mile Appalachian Trail than in the rest of the country. And yet, nine seems like nine too many. There should be no bloodshed on such hallowed ground—which is maybe why the murder of Winans and Williams seemed to tarnish the area.

An investigation of the double homicide revealed that neither of the women put up much of a fight—leading some to believe that maybe they had known the killer. Or maybe they had met him or her on the trail and linked itineraries, trusting that he or she was just another person outside experiencing Mother Nature's healing power. Whatever happened, Winans and Williams were victims of a puzzling crime, and no one has been charged. Who knows if it would be more settling if the case were finally closed, but still, to this day, thru-hikers report an odd feeling of being watched when they duck through the treed corridors of the Appalachian Trail in Shenandoah. The old hemlocks, some of which have been around for more than half of a century, have witnessed at least one tragedy, and maybe more.

DO IT

Section hike the Appalachian Trail from the famous Skyland Lodge south to Big Meadows on a 7-miler. From the Stony Man parking lot (38.593230, -78.375787), you can head south on the bridle path Winans and Williams took, but we recommend staying on the AT (prettier, less horse poop). Near mile 0.8 on the AT, you can split left onto the Whiteoak Canyon Trail; if you take this path 2 miles southeast, you'll end up within spitting distance of Winans's and Williams's campsite. (Connect the White Oak Fire Road and Skyline Drive to get back on the AT; this detour adds about 4.5 miles to the trip.) Leave a car at Big Meadows Campground (38.529182, -78.434067) or plan on retracing your steps to the Stony Man parking lot.

Midwest

Human Sacrifice

Mound 72, Nature/Culture Trail,
Cahokia Mounds State Historic Site, Illinois

THERE ONCE existed a people who built pyramids so tall, each one seemed to kiss the sky. They designed solar observatories to study the world that they lived in. They created an advanced network of villages around a fertile valley and cultivated corn and amaranth and seeds. And they subscribed to a belief that involved ritual human sacrifice—a lot of it. But you won't find evidence of their past in Mesopotamia, the Nile valley, Syria, South America, or even Central America. To walk among their history, you must go to southern Illinois.

One of the best-kept archaeological secrets of our world, let alone our country, Cahokia was a city of some 20,000 people that flourished in the Mississippi Valley from around AD 600 to AD 1400. St. Louisans know the area is special, but it does seem an odd location for such an advanced settlement. Consider, though, that the Illinois, Mississippi, and Missouri Rivers meet nearby, and the floodplain is especially fertile. And so that's where the Cahokians built a city of earthen mounds—square-bottomed, flat-topped pyramids—that we can explore today.

Park historians like to point out the mounds and explain how they're physical evidence of how advanced the Cahokians were. They'll tell you how they served as pedestals, the higher mounds reserved for the more important citizens. Monks Mound is some 10 stories tall, covering more than 13 acres. "It was a vital temple," or, "It was where the highest chief resided," they'll tell you. It's worth visiting, sure. But you won't get the same story if you visit Mound 72.

When archaeologists excavated Mound 72, they found more than 250 human skeletons. But the ridgetop mound was not just any burial ground: It was where humans were sacrificed. Scientists discovered four male skeletons that were linked arm in arm, but they were each missing hands and heads. Their skulls were arranged in a line nearby on a platform. Next, they found a mass grave of more than fifty females, ranging in age from fifteen to thirty, who showed signs of strangulation. Another mass grave within the mound hid thirty-nine skeletons, some of which were missing skulls and others of which had fractured skulls. And that's not even the worst of it: "From the vertical position of [their] fingers, which appear to have been digging in the sand, it is apparent that not all of the victims were dead when they were interred—that some had been trying to pull themselves out of the mass of bodies," wrote two archaeologists in *Cahokia, the Great Native American Metropolis.*

If cemeteries are unanimously creepy, then mass graves of murder victims are altogether disturbing—but you won't find that on the Cahokia brochure.

DO IT

You owe it to yourself to check out all of the earthwork at Cahokia, and the Nature/Culture Trail will touch most of the highlights in a 6.2-mile circuit. From the parking lot (38.654172, -90.058643), do the loop clockwise: Pass the Twin Mounds right away, then come up on Mound 72 near mile 0.5. Continue around past Woodhenge, a timber circle à la Stonehenge, before reaching Monks Mound and closing the loop.

Take Names

Neglige Lake, Moose Lake Entry Point #25, Boundary Waters Canoe Area Wilderness, Minnesota

WHOEVER IS responsible for assigning official names to places and landmarks must have had a time with Boundary Waters. The 1.3-million-acre tract of wilderness boasts more than 1,000 lakes— that's the highest concentration of lakes in the country. They range in size from 10 acres to 10,000 acres and, for the most part, they're named. Scan an index, and the rationale behind most names will be obvious, be it location (North and Western), size (Big and Short), or shape (Arc and Dogleg). Some sound like places you want to visit (Ecstasy and Hug), and some don't (Mosquito and No Sleep). And then there's Neglige Lake.

There's a lot of speculation as to how this 0.6-mile-long finger lake on the border earned its moniker, but one popular story suggests that there was a lumberjack in the late 1800s who ran a logging camp by Vera Lake, just north of present-day Neglige. He was a cutthroat boss, who'd fire his employees with the emotional dettachment of someone from *The Sopranos* and had no shame in stiffing any of his guys. More than that, though, he had a reputation for hitting the bottle.

The old lumberjack had fostered some sort of romantic relationship with a local Ojibwe girl by the time his logging business really took off. She was a lot younger than he, and probably smitten. He would buy her gifts of lingerie and make sure everyone knew she was his, which, to a certain degree, she probably enjoyed. But, as the story goes, one day the girl didn't come home. She was missing for a number of days before two

Ojibwe men found her floating face down in the finger lake south of Vera. Her head had been smashed in with the butt of an axe and her yellow, lacy negligée was stained red with blood.

The Ojibwe knew the old lumberjack had something to do with it, so they tracked him down and held a trial right there, beneath the jack pines. He was too drunk to come up with any sort of plausible alibi and ultimately admitted that he'd murdered the girl in his anger. The Ojibwe men stripped him down to his skivvies and hanged him from a tree, to dangle above Neglige Lake to his death.

DO IT

You don't have to paddle Boundary Waters, but that's certainly how the area has made a name for itself, so do it right: Launch from Moose Lake (47.987252, -91.500183) and string together Moose, Newfound, and Ensign Lakes (bass fishing here), about 11 miles. Portage about 0.5 mile east into Vera Lake. The easiest way into Neglige is via Trader Lake, so continue all the way across Vera to the 0.15-mile portage into Trader. Loop back west in your boat to the 0.2-mile portage into Neglige (brookies here). The lumberjack was supposedly hanged from a tree at the end of this portage. All in all, it's about 14 miles of paddling and portaging to Neglige. Nab a lakeside campsite in Vera if you wish to turn it into an overnight before heading back out the way you came.

The Sentinel

Wildcat Mountain, Old Settlers Trail, Wildcat Mountain State Park, Wisconsin

P EOPLE CAN'T agree on whose treasure is buried on the hemlock-shrouded slopes of Wildcat Mountain, nor can they agree on who—or what—is guarding it. But there *is* treasure and it *is* guarded.

Option A is that the notorious outlaw Jesse James came riding through this part of Wisconsin after the Civil War, robbing banks and raiding stagecoaches. He made a quick fortune, but ran into trouble south of the Twin Cities in Northfield, Minnesota, in 1876. Some combination of the nefarious James-Younger Gang demanded money from a local bank, but townspeople caught on fast. Locals came pouring in, shooting at the outlaws, and forcing them out of town. So the six surviving criminals split up and fled. Some were cornered and some were sentenced, but not the James brothers; the two outlaws escaped from Minnesota and headed east for Nashville—but legend has it that they made a pitstop.

The boys, knowing that they were likely being tracked by law enforcement and citizens alike, decided to hide their spoils, or at least that's how the legend goes. They rode into Wisconsin and came upon the present-day Wildcat Mountain State Park. A rare driftless region in the Midwest, the area would have looked (and still looks) markedly different than other topography in Wisconsin. Because it was shaped by wind and precipitation, rather than glacial activity, the terrain is severe: Steep bluffs and ravines scar pristine forests, and the rock is pockmarked with springs, caves, and sinkholes. It would have been as good a hiding spot as any, and so the James brothers buried their gold and contraband somewhere on Wildcat Mountain.

Option B is that the governor of Illinois in the late 1890s had connections to a particularly big fortune that, for some reason, was in Billings, Montana. The governor, John Peter Altgeld, organized its return to Chicago, but word escaped that there was a gold-filled wagon scraping its way east—and, as we know from Option A, it was not a safe time on the roads. As the rickety wagon bumped through present-day Wildcat Mountain State Park, someone in on the mission ordered that the treasure be hidden for safekeeping.

Now it is, of course, possible that both fortunes remain hidden somewhere among the rocky recesses and groves of pines and hemlocks—but neither has been found. At least one is guarded by what locals have called the "Sentinel." Some people have described seeing a very real-looking man in late-1800s period clothing; sometimes he's on horseback, and he's often carrying a fixed-blade knife or a rifle. Sometimes he throws rocks or sticks to frighten treasure-seekers. On the other hand, some hikers have described an unnatural wildcat. Sometimes it's the size of a housecat, but other times it's the size of a car. It prowls the wooded slopes, but doesn't show up in photographs. Though, if the Sentinel is a shapeshifter, every theory suddenly has merit.

DO IT

From the Amphitheater Parking Lot (43.701782, -90.570556), take the access spur to the 2.5-mile Old Settlers Trail. The path loops counterclockwise through pine woods and past overlooks of the valley below. The park doesn't offer reenactments (at this time), so anyone dressed in period clothing is either a creep or the Sentinel. It would be rare to spot a bobcat and miraculous to see any other type of wildcat, so also probably the Sentinel.

Breathe Easy

Wind Cave, Wild Cave Tour,
Wind Cave National Park, South Dakota

TOM AND Jesse Bingham were a couple of simple cowboys who roamed the badlands of the Dakota Territory in the late 1800s. They likely knew the folds of the Black Hills, where vast grasslands abut emerald-carpeted hills shocked with granite, better than any hiker can claim today. But there's a lot to the area that doesn't meet the eye.

One day in 1881, the two brothers were riding through present-day western South Dakota, tracking game. They followed a wounded deer up a draw when one of the brothers heard a distinct whistle pierce the otherwise quiet landscape. He hopped off his horse and followed the noise to a small opening in the rock where he believed the hissing was coming from. As he peered inside, a powerful gust burst from the hole, blowing his hat clean off his head. It was as though Mother Earth had taken a deep breath.

We know now that there's a scientific explanation for the phenomenon—differences in barometric pressure between the cave and the outside cause air to rush to the lower of the two—but that's about all we know. That small hole in the rock that the Bingham brothers stumbled upon is like a geological Pandora's box. There are the small wonders, like why, when stalactites and stalagmites are so commonplace in limestone caves across the globe, are they so rare in Wind Cave? Or, on the other hand, why does ultra-rare boxwork, a formation where the veins of calcite permeate outward like a giant spiderweb, form in absolute abundance in this cave? Then there are the bigger curiosities, like just how huge is it? Experts have mapped more than 140 miles of passages in Wind Cave's belly, but

surely there are more—right? In a time when humans know so much about the world we live in, Wind Cave remains a relative mystery.

The Binghams, the story goes, returned to show off the mysterious blowhole to some peers some days later. But this time, when one stuck his head near the opening, a violent gust sucked his hat inside the dark maw. The two thought better about retrieving the hat, and it's just as well: Mother Earth will return it when the time is right.

DO IT

The only way to explore Wind Cave is on a guided tour. The Natural Entrance Tour, which runs approximately 0.7 mile, is best for families. More adventurous folks should try the Wild Cave Tour, which avoids the developed paths in favor of tight, dark passages (read: crawling required). All tours begin from the visitor center (43.556223, -103.478122).

Lady of the Dunes

Lake Michigan, Dune Succession Trail,
Indiana Dunes National Lakeshore, Indiana

I
T'S HARD to imagine a piece of wilderness that looks more out of place than the 15,000-acre expanse of dunes nestled amid the unbroken jungle of asphalt and steel that links Chicago, Gary, and Michigan City. The Indiana Dunes, a 15-mile-long piece of protected shoreline on the southernmost tip of cerulean Lake Michigan, are just that. Formed over thousands of years, they soar more than a hundred feet over the water before giving way to a patchwork of hardwoods, wetlands, and prairies. It's a refuge for urbanites, and of the handful of people responsible for leading the conservation efforts to protect them, you can thank at least one when you visit.

Alice Gray came to live on the dunes in 1915 at the age of thirty-four. She was a feminist, ahead of her time, and disenchanted with society. She wasn't a drifter or a hermit, like some of the folks who squatted on the scenic shoreline, and rather came from money and graduated with honors from the University of Chicago. She moved to Germany after graduating, where she discovered something that resembled Buddhism, then came home, worked for an astronomy publication, and gave it up for a life on the dunes. Unlike the others who passed through, she stuck around and survived harsh winters in a crude shelter made of driftwood. She was, at one time, quoted in an old periodical as having said that she survived for years on the dunes on her final paycheck, her only expenses being bread and salt.

At the time, industry was growing, and steel-mill and power-plant developers had no qualms in sourcing from the dunes. Hoosier Slide, for instance, was a 200-foot-tall dune and the area's largest—but it no longer exists. Major glass makers carried it away in railroad boxcars. And so Gray, arguably the area's most knowledgeable and passionate advocate, fought for the dunes' protection at a time when conservation wasn't a buzzword and certainly wasn't in vogue.

While she was lobbying, she was, of course, living. She subsisted on the land, supposedly harvesting plants and hunting small game, and had no need for societal norms. Allegedly, fishermen caught on and began spying on the woman as she gallivanted along the shore without clothes. On at least one occasion, she was seen bathing in Lake Michigan.

While Gray was alive to see the area recognized as a state park, she, unfortunately, passed away before part of it was declared a national lakeshore in the 1960s. Her obituary called her a "woman who, though a college graduate, forsook the society of humans for the solitude of the dunes...." But, perhaps she remains as much a part of the Indiana Dunes as they did of her: Visitors to the area have claimed to see the ghost of a naked woman wandering across the white-sand beaches or disappearing into the water.

DO IT

The best hiking trails to the dunes are within the West Beach trail system (the area is divided into fifteen disconnected sections). From the parking lot (41.620294, -87.209097), combine the three loops into a 3.5-mile circuit. The Dune Succession Trail takes you through the stages of dune development as it transports you to a vantage over Lake Michigan; the West Beach Loop tracks through loose sand along Long Lake; and the Long Loop Trail moves from its namesake up into the dunes. Alice Gray's ghost is most often spotted beneath the moonlight, so time your trip when you can camp at one of the twelve walk-in sites at Dunewood (nps. gov/indu); the park closes to day visitors at 6 p.m.

Murder, She Wrote

St. Louis Canyon, St. Louis Canyon Trail, Starved Rock State Park, Illinois

THE FLURRIES of snow fluttered earthward, sparkling and dancing in the still night. It was one of those dreamy storms that sets a city afresh and covers its blemishes, the kind that you see in the movies. By the morning of March 16, 1960, a foot of white blanketed Chicago and its angular turrets and shining steel—and one of the state's most heinous crimes.

Eighty miles away, just beyond the city's western suburbs, three women lay slain beneath the snow. They were friends—wives of Chicago corporate executives, mothers of older children, and active members of their local church—who'd escaped the suburban hustle for a four-day trip to Starved Rock, arguably the state's best and most scenic park. Located on the southern banks of the mighty Illinois River, the park is home to a handful of sandstone canyons and caves, waves of colorful hardwoods, and a bounty of easy-access buttes that overlook the valley. It's a rare slice of wilderness so close to a major city.

Lillian Oetting, Frances Murphy, and Mildred Lindquist checked into the lodge in the afternoon of Monday, March 14, then, donning galoshes and oversized wool coats, set out to explore St. Louis Canyon. One of the park's marquee box canyons, the sandstone amphitheater is less than 2 miles from the visitor center. At its head, a ribbon of water spills more than 50 feet over the sandstone into a circular basin. At the time, it was frozen, a bubble gum-blue sheet of ice, terracing to the canyon floor. Shortly after arriving at the icefall, or perhaps on their return, the women were brutally murdered. The killer dragged the bodies aside, toward a shelf of sandstone and off the beaten path, and left. Two days passed before investigators uncovered the corpses from the snow and began to piece together the evidence. (A man was convicted and is presently serving a life sentence.)

But, if local lore is to be believed, the horrid triple homicide at Starved Rock may not even be the state park's worst. Consider its name: Legend has it that in April 1769, nearly two centuries before the murders, as many as 2,000 Illini were cornered atop a sandstone pinnacle on the Illinois River by the Ottawas and Pottawatomies. Some escaped, some were slain, and some jumped to their deaths, but most of them starved to death on the outcropping.

Nowadays, hikers still flock to Starved Rock like Oetting, Murphy, and Lindquist did in 1960. They still set out to see the box canyons that the Illinois River has bored over thousands of years, and they still venture out to the buttes that rise a hundred feet from the Illinois River. But now, some report hearing wails and groans echoing through the canyons. We know of at least 2,003 possibilities why.

DO IT

Park at the lodge (41.318048, -88.993125) and you'll be in prime position to tackle any of Starved Rock's trails, which spider out from here. To visit St. Louis Canyon, link the Bluff and St. Louis Canyon Trails roughly 1.5 miles to reach the sandstone amphitheater. You can drive closer, but then you'll miss out on Aurora, Sac, and Kickapoo Canyons, worthy destinations in their own rights. Retrace your steps by the same route on the return. Starved Rock, the park's namesake and supposed location of the trapped Illini, is an easy, 0.3-mile walk north from the lodge toward the river.

History Repeats Itself

Devil's Lake, Ice Age National Scenic Trail, Devil's Lake State Park, Wisconsin

ON A COOL fall morning, the mist drifts over the rock walls, twisting through the red oaks and maples and hanging over the slate-colored water. The screech of a loon cuts through the solitude, echoing off the quartzite. The bow of an old aluminum canoe slices through the water, flaying the mist and creating a triangular wake. And then, stillness.

Hemmed in by towering quartzite formations on all sides, Devil's Lake has no inlet or outlet—it's been the same since the last ice age—which, in itself, is mysterious. No wonder the place is the subject of so many eerie folk tales, not the least of which is the phantom canoe, which regularly makes appearances at twilight.

There are the elaborate effigy mounds on the north shore—clear indications that prehistoric people believed the pool sacred. Then there's the collection of Ho-Chunk legends. The tribespeople, which began calling the pool Spirit Lake, tell origin tales of water spirits and thunderbirds, explaining the odd rock formations here and around the Dells.

White settlers changed the name to Devil's Lake along the way, which seems to suit. By the twentieth century, campers began complaining about large, shadowy figures rustling outside their tents. Rumors have floated of flesh-eating maggots in the water. Someone snapped a photo of a cat-like, serpentine lake monster. Recreationists have perished, either by drowning or by falling from rock walls, leading to the lake's nickname as the "place of the many dead." Paranormal investigators have tallied readings from the shore as recently as 2012.

The phantom canoe may just be the one constant in the lake's history.

DO IT

Check off one of the 1,200-mile Ice Age National Scenic Trail's best sections on the 11-mile horseshoe-shaped bit that loops around Devil's Lake. From the STH-113 northern trailhead (43.424695, -89.685699), take the Ice Age Trail west around Devil's Lake and back, ending at the STH-113 southern trailhead (43.405748, -89.675746). Leave a shuttle car at the southern parking area, or plan to add a 1.5-mile road walk to complete the loop. The middle 3 or so miles of this route circle Devil's Lake along its western bluffs.

Look Alive

South Manitou Island, Shoreline Route, Sleeping Bear Dunes National Lakeshore, Michigan

We had no intention of landing at South Manitou, but we were now little more than a floating dead-house, and we landed there to bury our dead . . . We dug a long trench on the beach, and buried the twenty dead emigrants just as they had died, without coffin or preacher.

—Hon. George W. Gardner, 18509

A T FIRST glance, there's really nothing all that spooky about the Manitou. Granted, they do look out of place, islands you'd be more likely find in the tropics than Lake Michigan, but that enhances their charm. Turquoise water rims white-sand beaches, deer lope across the shores, overgrown trails wind through pine woods—the twin islands are like settings you might see in a children's movie. Even their origin story, per the Chippewa, is a cute tale of a mama bear and two cubs.

But their idyllic appearance masks a frightening truth: The Manitou are death traps. Consider that there are more than fifty known shipwrecks blanketing the floor of Lake Michigan in the Manitou Passage alone. Though the Manitou are 7 miles off the coast of Sleeping Bear Dunes in west Michigan, the navigable passage is estimated at less than a mile wide. If Chicago-bound ships deviate from the deep-water strait even slightly, hidden shoals seem to snatch them and drag them to the depths. There are so many wrecks in this area, in fact, that it's been protected as an underwater preserve for divers—a ship graveyard.

Stories of divers' encounters with ghosts and the paranormal in the Manitou Passage Underwater Preserve litter the Internet, but perhaps more alarming are the reports from hikers who've claimed to hear the desperate cries of phantom people drowning off the shores of South Manitou. Throw in the suspicion that the South Manitou light tower is supposedly haunted by its former keeper, and the fact that the island is essentially a 3.5-by-3-mile burial ground almost seems fitting.

Of course, it should be noted that not only did 1800s steamers pull ashore at South Manitou to bury their passengers who had succumbed to cholera, they also buried those who were afflicted but not yet dead. That's right: They buried people dead and alive. So it shouldn't be all that surprising that these ghosts are so restless that people have reported seeing them literally rising from their graves and walking along the white-sand beaches, turquoise waves licking their toes.

DO IT

Buy a round-trip ferry ticket to South Manitou from Leland (manitoutransit.com) and make it worth your while with a 12-mile, 3-day trip. From the harbor at Sandy Point (45.012186, -86.094621), head 3.7 miles inland past a mass grave and 1800s-era homesteads and cemeteries to the Popple Campground on the island's northern tip. Next, head out to the beach and follow the shore counterclockwise around South Manitou and past the *Francisco Morazan* shipwreck to the Weather Station Campground, 7 miles away. Day 3, close the loop about 1.3 miles to the boathouse and catch your ferry home.

The Writing on the Wall

Conkles Hollow, Conkles Hollow Gorge Trail, Conkles Hollow State Nature Preserve, Ohio

IT'S A SHAME that so few people know of the Buckeye State's most spectacular gorge, but in a region that's filled with them, one rises to the top—literally. Conkles Hollow features walls of black, striated sandstone that loom 200 feet above the valley of waterfalls like sentinels. The area is so densely packed with birches and hemlocks, however, that the gorge remains relatively hidden. Aerial images make it look more like a putting green than a chasm, which is just as well: Maybe the treasure that's tucked in the recesses of the rock isn't supposed to be found.

See, there are questions about its origin and its rightful owner. According to local lore, a flotilla of settlers was rafting down the Ohio River when it was ambushed by a band of Shawnee people. The Native Americans looted the boats and robbed the men and then hightailed it north to the Hocking Hills in the south-central part of present-day Ohio. Concerned that they were being pursued, they decided to hide their spoils in a narrow chasm. At the head of this deep-sided hollow, they laid a towering hemlock like a ladder. One of the men climbed to the top, then hid the money in a small pockmark, while the others etched an arrow on the eastern wall that pointed to the western wall and the booty. Then they left.

Some people say that the Natives never returned for money, and others suggest that time and storms knocked over the remaining hemlocks near the treasure, preventing them from accessing it, but most agree that it remains. The arrow etching has since faded, but it may not have helped, anyway: Hikers have reported hearing chanting and shouting in the narrow gorge, the supposed ghosts of Shawnee tribespeople guarding their treasure. Or perhaps searching for it.

DO IT

First, check out the inside: Take the Conkles Hollow Gorge Trail to the amphitheater where a waterfall plunges over the sandstone and where the treasure is likely hidden, then retrace your steps for a 1.5-mile out-and-back. Next, see the outside: Follow the Rim Trail, which circles the gorge in a 2.5-mile loop. Both paths start from the same parking lot and trailhead (39.452996, -82.572105).

The River Monster

TRUE, NORTH Dakota's winters are the stuff of legends. But those single-digit temperatures give way to spring eventually, and for that, we have a different legend to thank, sort of. Early natives to the area believed that the Miniwashitu was responsible for spring's coming on, but while the creature serves a sort of groundhog-like duty in the country's northernmost regions, it's no cuddly rodent. "Miniwashitu" translates loosely to "water monster" in the native Mandan language.

Miniwashitu is, in fact, massive. Early periodicals from the North Dakota State Historical Society describe a "most dreadful" creature: ". . . it was of strange form and covered all over with hair like a buffalo, but red in color; it had only one eye in the middle of its forehead, and above that a single horn. Its backbone stood out notched and jagged like an enormous saw."[10] Imagine such a monster, a giant, red, one-eyed bison with spikes, plowing through the ice in the Little Missouri, and that's the Miniwashitu.

According to old Mandan written history, the Miniwashitu lumbers upstream, bulldozing the ice and spurring on the spring melt. But its work is sacred, in a sense, and not fit for human eyes. Stories tell of unfortunate souls who glimpsed the beast before going crazy, losing their eyesight, and falling terminally ill. The only time when it's safe to watch the Miniwashitu at work is at night: It's said to glow red like a flame as it moves against the current, roaring with a deafening tone.

Campers today may not spot the Miniwashitu, but as long as spring returns, maybe that's not such a bad thing.

DO IT

It's unfortunate that the place that spurred on its namesake's conservation efforts (where "the romance of my life began," Teddy wrote later) is such an unsung spot in our national parks system, but that spells solitude for intrepid hikers. Tackle the seldom-visited North Unit on a 19-mile loop around a section of the Little Missouri: From the Juniper Campground (47.593995, -103.335278), make a clockwise circuit by connecting the Achenbach, North Achenbach, and Buckhorn Trails. Throw down on a mud bench overlooking the river near mile 7, where you're all but guaranteed views of badlands, bison, the Milky Way, and, maybe, the Miniwashitu.

The Revenant

Scotts Bluff, North Overlook Trail, Scotts Bluff National Monument, Nebraska

IRAM SCOTT was the sort of man whose life would lend itself nicely to a silver-screen blockbuster. He was a fur trader in the early nineteenth century, which meant that he had the adventurous spirit and brave countenance of a pioneer and the physical fortitude and general ability of a trapper. Indeed, the young man was tall enough and muscular enough that old texts mention both as defining characteristics. Early drawings depict a man with a square jaw and broad shoulders proportionate to the Oscar statuette.

In the late 1820s, Scott and a small band of traders headed out west to track muskrats, rabbits, and beavers. They intended to catch and skin the animals for their pelts, which could be brought back to St. Louis and sold to buyers in the bustling East Coast metropolises, but Scott also knew of an easier way. This isn't to say he was cutting corners, but Scott understood the trading game better than anyone. Instead of putting all of his time and resources into hunting game, he could simply track a tribe of Native Americans and trade them manufactured goods, like axes or knives, for their already-trapped game. It was Economics 101 in 1828.

That year, Scott and his caravan likely did business with the Blackfeet in the Great Plains before turning around. With Scott at the head and the trapped and purchased pelts in tow, the crew made its way back east to St. Louis. They rode along the Oregon Trail, the historic, 2,170-mile route from the Pacific Northwest to the Missouri River valley, wending through the alternating open plains and castle-like rock features. The mixed sandstone and limestone formations of the high plains have been weathered over millennia into stark faces and mesas that soar hundreds of feet above the grassy flatlands. It wouldn't have been a bad place to stop and rest for a bit.

And, unfortunately, that was Scott's fate. It's unclear why, but the leader was abandoned somewhere along the banks of the North Platte River, likely in the high plains of eastern Wyoming. Some old texts suggest that he had fallen ill, while others say he was gravely injured after a dispute with the Blackfeet, but either way, his caravan believed he could no longer continue, and so they left him for dead, not unlike the plot of a recent award-winning film.

And, as in that flick, Scott pressed on. The man, believed to be in his early- or mid-twenties at the time—crawled, clawed, and inched his way some 100 miles east to the land of bluffs and caprocks in present-day western Nebraska. It was there, near an 800-foot-tall wall of rock, that trappers later found the man's skeleton. He had traveled a miraculous distance, given the circumstances, and had even crossed the river in order to die beneath the bluffs. There was something about them; perhaps their unflashy grandeur seemed to mirror the man himself, but he was attracted to them—and may have never left. The trapper has been spotted flickering among the shadows of the rocks and lingering by the water in the monument's northern fringes. He may have been left for dead, but it seems he remains in spirit.

DO IT

Hop on the 0.5-mile out-and-back North Overlook Trail from the summit parking lot (41.836644, -103.700220). The short walk leads to a promontory, a peninsula in the sky, overlooking the river valley where Scott likely succumbed to his illness or injuries. To make the trip longer, you can tack on the 1.6-mile Saddle Rock Trail, which meanders down past various rock formations to the visitor center.

A Stranger Among Us

Mark Twain Cave, Mark Twain Cave Tour, Hannibal, Missouri

This main avenue was not more than eight or ten feet wide. Every few steps other lofty and still narrower crevices branched from it on either hand—for [the] cave was but a vast labyrinth of crooked aisles that ran into each other and out again and led nowhere. It was said that one might wander days and nights together through its intricate tangle of rifts and chasms, and never find the end of the cave; and that he might go down, and down, and still down, into the earth, and it was just the same—labyrinth under labyrinth, and no end to any of them. No man "knew" the cave. That was an impossible thing. Most of the young men knew a portion of it, and it was not customary to venture much beyond this known portion. Tom Sawyer knew as much of the cave as any one.[11]

THOUGH THIS subterranean maze on the banks of the Mississippi has a long history of capturing imaginations, fictional it is not. First, Native Americans discovered its whereabouts and used it, presumably, as a warm refuge in the winter. A local hunter stumbled upon its maw while tracking a panther in the early 1800s. Thereafter, Jesse James hid out in its shadowy depths, and draft dodgers evaded the Civil War in its underground passages. More skeletons have been found in its folds than can be identified. But, perhaps the most notable story of the cave begins in 1848, when it landed in the possession of Dr. Joseph Nash McDowell via a land grant.

The surgeon believed the solitude and constant 52 degrees Fahrenheit air temperatures would be perfect for his work—of preserving dead bodies. So one can only imagine what a young Samuel Clemens thought when he peeled around a corner in a dank corridor within the cave's belly to come face to face with a suspended corpse, dangling from the ceiling. She was a young girl, about fourteen, and she was inside a copper-lined glass tube that was filled with alcohol, bobbing in the fluid—the sort of sight that you just can't erase from a young boy's mind. The experience would color the graveyard scene in *The Adventures of Tom Sawyer*, and the cave itself would, of course, become a central setting in the book.

Dr. McDowell had tried to petrify his daughter, who'd passed away from pneumonia some time earlier. But by the time local kids discovered the room of the dead, he was forced to remove all corpses from his cave. Dr. McDowell and his daughter are now buried at the family mausoleum in St. Louis, but perhaps his daughter never truly left.

Visitors to the cave have reported seeing a young, pretty girl hiding among its shadows. She's often seen wearing a long, period-style dress with a high collar and a shawl, but when spoken to, she either vanishes or turns away and walks into one of the never-ending chambers. Others, including guides, have said that they feel a distinct heaviness in the air or a chill down their backs when they're inside the cave, and many refuse to enter alone—even if they'll have company upon entering.

DO IT

The 6.5-mile-long cave is privately owned, so you must go on a guided tour to explore it. The Mark Twain Cave Tour is offered year-round (marktwaincave.com) and should take around one hour. Find parking off Cave Hollow Road via MO 79 (39.688877, -91.331974).

Shutter Island

Isle Royale, Greenstone Ridge Trail, Isle Royale National Park, Michigan

THE THICK forest of spruces drapes off the ridge, almost down to the shore, where waves lap against the rocky coast. A wind whips across the water, whistling through the quivering trees, and then stillness. A thick, damp chill settles over the scene before a shrill howl pierces the air. If you weren't asleep yet, chances are good you won't be for the rest of the night. Welcome to Isle Royale.

Isle Royale is lonely by nature, surrounded by the frigid waters of Lake Superior and only accessible via a seven-hour ferry ride, which makes it bucket-list worthy for backpackers if only for its inherent solitude. But there's a flip side to all that seclusion. The mind is wont to take over.

That's what happened to Charlie Mott more than 150 years ago. As the story goes, he and his wife, Alice, were hired to guard a copper mine on Isle Royale in 1845. They were dropped off with enough supplies to last two weeks, but their resupply boat never returned. They allegedly survived on tree bark and berries for half a year before Charlie went mad. Driven by the acutest hunger, he tried to slaughter his wife with a butcher knife, Alice later told authorities. He didn't succeed, and he died some days later. After Alice was eventually rescued, she alleged that Charlie had died of natural causes, but confessed that she had considered making a bone broth from his remains.

Whether she killed him or not, Alice's story (and Charlie's, for that matter) wasn't unique. In fact, craving human flesh in dire times was apparently a common enough occurrence that it already had a name: the Wendigo. The Algonquian people of America's northernmost reaches contended that an evil spirit called the Wendigo corrupted weak-minded

people, turning their hearts to ice and, among other things, giving them an insatiable craving for human flesh.

Since the 1600s, people have told stories of the Wendigo. They even hosted something resembling the American witch trials against people accused of being possessed by it in the early 1900s. It seems rash, perhaps a low point in North American history, if only because we've all been there. We've not necessarily experienced cannibalistic urges, but everyone who's hiked has dealt with hunger, to a degree. Setting off into the woods, carrying everything you plan to eat is primal and part of the allure of hiking—but you're never farther from your next meal than you are on Isle Royale.

Better not miss your return ferry.

DO IT

A one-way ferry ticket to Isle Royale from Grand Portage can be pricey, so get your money's worth by spending up to a week traversing the island east to west on a 42-mile epic. Take the *Voyageur II* (isleroyaleboats.com) to the trailhead (48.158908, -88.471938) at Rock Harbor. Look south to Mott Island, where Charlie and Alice watched over the mine and allegedly considered eating one another. Pick up the Greenstone Ridge Trail and follow Isle Royale's backbone west above the carpet of spruce, passing idyllic lakeside campsites as you work your way to the Windingo (yup) trailhead at Washington Harbor. Isle Royale is the Lower 48's least-visited national park, so expect solitude, but keep an eye on your tentmate.

King of the Hills

Coronado Heights Castle, Coronado Heights Park Trail, Coronado Heights Park, Kansas

I T WAS once believed that there existed seven opulent cities of gold. They were magical lands, filled with riches and spoils, and, essentially, up for the taking. In the 1500s, Spanish colonial officials in Mexico City got it in their heads that these lands—the Seven Cities of Cíbola—were somewhere north, scattered about the desert like mystical oases. A friar backed them up, saying he had seen such a city on his travels through the New World. "It is situated on a level stretch on the brow of a roundish hill," [12] he claimed. "It appears to be a very beautiful city, the best that I have seen in these parts." And that's how Francisco Vázquez de Coronado ended up in Kansas.

The conquistador led a brigade of Spanish soldiers and Native American guides north into the New World in search of the fabled Seven Cities of Cíbola, which per the friar, they believed might be in present-day central Kansas. They traveled some 4,000 miles around the American West before landing upon a sandstone bluff that rose 300 feet out of the prairie. It wasn't made of gold, but it must have been a welcome sight because the relentlessly optimistic Coronado wrote to the king, "The country itself is the best I have ever seen for producing all the products of Spain, for besides the land itself being . . . well watered by the rivulets and springs and rivers, I found prunes like those of Spain, and nuts, and very good sweet grapes, and mulberries. . . ." [13]

Coronado and his men spent nearly a month in Kansas before determining that it was not fit for a Spanish settlement (too far from the ocean and too cold in wintertime). So, two years after they set out on this expedition, the ragtag team returned to Mexico City empty-handed.

Instead of conceding that the Seven Cities of Cíbola were fabled, however, Spanish officials simply determined that Coronado had failed in his mission. The undeserved scapegoat, Coronado never overcame the debt he'd accrued while on his expedition through the West, which maybe he still believes unfair.

Today, hikers have reported seeing inexplicable movements in the grasses below the limestone castle in the center of the park. Erected by the Works Progress Administration in the 1930s, the castle is a cool structure and offers a top-of-the-world view over the surrounding prairie—but is potentially built on top of a burial ground. Some guests believe that the men who died on Coronado's expedition were interred somewhere around here, so perhaps their spirits are restless. One wonders though, whether after his unceremonious return to Mexico City, Coronado eventually decided Kansas was a fit after all.

DO IT

Drive to the top of the hillock and park near the castle (38.613182, -97.703229). From there, explore the castle and nab the vantage overlooking the prairie (pay attention to weird rustling). Then, explore the park by foot on the 3.2-mile Coronado Heights Park Trail, which loops around the hill, passing spiderwort and butterfly milkweed. There are supposedly plums and berries around here that are as good as those in Spain (typically fruiting July through September).

Higher Power

Effigy Mounds, South Unit Trails, Effigy Mounds National Monument, Iowa

THE WINDING timeline of humans didn't bypass America—we just never hear about it. That makes sense: Western civilization and culture are borne from ancient communities in and around the Middle East, so that's what we study. But imagine if axes were reversed and we grew and adapted from the ancient people who thrived around the Mississippi River valley some 1,600 years ago. Things would certainly look different.

We don't know much about these folks, but they left their marks, literally. These people, or at least the ones we know about, were mound builders, people who manipulated the earth into shapes and structures. It's not totally clear why they did this, but we have a pretty good idea, for instance, that the community near present-day St. Louis used mounds to delineate the various castes—and to bury people. (Turn to the Human Sacrifice chapter on page 101 to read more about these people.)

But the ancient mound builders some 300 miles north as the crow flies didn't build pyramids or mass burials. Visit what's preserved of their civilization near the Yellow River State Forest and you'll spy "standard" burial mounds, sure. But among and around those conical mounds, you'll find effigies of bears and birds. These earthen shapes aren't tall—no more than 3 or 4 feet, in fact—nor are they receptacles for human remains, for the most part. The best we can figure is that they were central to various ceremonial rituals.

And from there, the mind reels. Were these people worshiping the creatures who were native to this land long before humans? Or were they asking for protection? (From what?) Or were they asking to be brought back to this earth after death in the form of an animal? Or, consider that the shapes are best discerned when looking down upon them with a bird's-eye vantage: Were they communicating to some avian or, weirder still, extraterrestrial race?

DO IT

The patchwork of trails at Effigy Mounds National Monument services all types of earthworks, no matter which you choose; the views of the Mississippi from the North Unit are best, but the effigies from the South Unit are better. For the latter, begin at the day-use area near 43.082156, -91.180375 (the North Unit trails begin at the visitor center), and string together the South Unit paths 2 miles to the Marching Bear Group, a collection of ten bear-shaped mounds where visitors have reported malfunctioning phones and cameras. Retrace your steps on the return, splitting off onto various spurs to see other earthworks.

The Lady in Black

Stepp Cemetery, Three Lakes Trail, Morgan-Monroe State Forest, Indiana

H IDDEN WITHIN the 24,000-acre Morgan-Monroe State Forest, shrouded in hardwoods and buffered by hollows, is a graveyard of some thirty headstones. You could hike past, undulating through the thick canopy, without noticing it at all, if not for the concrete sign: "Stepp Cemetery, Established Early 1800s." Behind the placard, a mixed forest is slowly overtaking what was once cleared, roots bursting through the headstones. It's what happens when man takes a swing at nature and nature fights back.

People set aside the area a few centuries ago for farming, but, unsurprisingly, it didn't work out. The alternating ridges and valleys are choked with rocks, and the clay didn't take seed anyway. By 1929, the state purchased the land for recreation and logging, and every settler had long since left—with the exception of the Lady in Black.

A holdover from the old days, the Lady in Black is the ghost of a woman with cascading white hair, a floor-length black gown, and, often, a veil. Hikers (and ghost hunters) have claimed to see her lurking in the cemetery and sitting on an old stump in the clearing. It has all the makings of a good, old-fashioned campfire story, and legitimate paranormal investigations back it up; scientists have captured footage of the area with stark audio anomalies and inexplicable amorphous clouds.

Legend has it that the Lady in Black was a dutiful homemaker in the early 1900s. She and her husband, a stonecutter at the local quarry, had one daughter, and the trio lived in a modest home amid the hemlocks and dogwoods. They didn't have much, but they had enough, the story goes.

But that all changed when tragedy struck: First, the husband was killed in an accident down at the quarry, and shortly thereafter, the daughter died in a car accident. The widow was driven mad by her grief and spent her final days weeping in the cemetery until she supposedly disappeared, never to be seen—in life—again.

DO IT

The best part about this hike is, of course, that even if you dispute the legend of the Lady in Black, you cannot deny the cemetery. It's there, trailside, headstones and all, in the middle of the Morgan-Monroe State Forest. The best way to see it is near the midway point of the 10-mile Three Lakes Trail, which actually passes two lakes, but is still a scenery-packed circuit. From the trailhead near Bryant Creek Lake (39.323081, -86.477004), circle counterclockwise through the hardwoods, following Hacker and Precinct Ridges. The cemetery will be on hiker's left after you cross Forest Road.

Mountain West

The Blue Mist

Mummy Range, Lawn Lake Trail,
Rocky Mountain National Park, Colorado

OLD MINER Bill was the village crazy person in Estes Park 100 years ago. Before that, he was a prospector who had moved out to southern Colorado in the 1880s to strike a fortune beneath the pinnacled skyline of the San Juans— but it never worked. He was a free spirit and talked of wild things, and, as far as the townspeople were concerned, put too much stock in the cosmos. People got to talking and before long, rumors ran rampant that Old Bill was insane. In 1904, the coot was sent to an asylum.

When the prospector was released later, he made his way north to try his hand at mining the glaciated peaks at the other end of the state—and that's how he ended up in Estes. He set to mining Horseshoe Park, a massive, verdant valley that's framed by snow-capped mountains, and then tried his luck on the higher slopes. He supposedly filed multiple claims on 12,454-foot Mt. Chapin, the southernmost tooth of the Mummy Range, and is even credited with establishing a footpath up to the high country that was later paved over as the Old Fall River Road.

But he was odd. When he came into town, he'd tell absurd stories of monsters and ghosts up in the mountains—or a blue mass of fog that he said appeared every so often above Horseshoe Park before drifting up the valley and disappearing. He told the townspeople he'd watch it from his cabin on Mt. Chapin and then hurtle down through the evergreens and aspens to take a closer look, only to find huge, cloven prints where the mist had been. They were far too big to be that of a moose or a buck, he said. And worse, he'd always find animal bones that had been picked clean strewn near the prints in the wake of the blue mist. Townspeople wrote

Old Miner Bill off, but still, it was an oddly specific story—and he told some version of it whenever he came off the mountain.

At some point, the people living in Estes realized they hadn't seen the old prospector in some time, so they sent a small party to go check on him. But when the villagers arrived at Miner Bill's cabin on the flanks of Mt. Chapin, all they found were a set of huge hoofprints and the prospector's remains.

DO IT

Hikers have reported seeing the eerie blue mist drift through valleys from a number of high points in the park, so no need to limit yourself. But the Mummies are both stunning and relatively quiet (by Front Range standards), so you might as well go straight to the source: Mt. Chapin. Easy option: From the parking lot off Fall River Road (40.407067, -105.626271), string together the Lawn Lake and Ypsilon Lake Trails 4.5 miles to camp near an alpine lake in the shadow of Chapin and a cast of toothy Thirteeners. Adventurer's option: From the Chapin Creek trailhead on Old Fall River Road (40.434646, -105.730196), walk up the western flank of Mt. Chapin on trail. Net the Twelver near mile 2, then go off trail to bag the rest of the Mummies. The route-finding is relatively straightforward, and ambitious hikers can tick off nine summits (all are walk-ups) on what locals call the 18-mile Grand Slam.

The Mountains
Are Calling

Seven Devils Mountains, Seven Devils Loop, Hells Canyon Wilderness, Idaho

H E DEVIL, She Devil, The Ogre, Devils Throne, The Goblin, the Twin Imps—if you didn't know better, they could be villains in a storybook, not 9,000-foot granite massifs. But, in a sense, the Seven Devils Mountains are both.

Tucked on the state line between Oregon and Idaho, the misshapen parapets of the Seven Devils appear less like majestic, snow-capped pinnacles than a dark, scabrous oil spill in the sky. The volcanic peaks are entirely out of place, rising above wildflower-studded meadows and jewel-like lakes, which is why the leading theory is that they were, at one time, a pack of child-eating giants.

The Nez Perce tell a legend of seven monsters that lived in the easternmost fringes of the Pacific Northwest's Blue Mountains long ago. They were "taller than the tallest pines and stronger than the strongest oaks,"[14] and, for what it's worth, feasted on young children. Each year, they descended from the mountains to hunt kids, and, eventually, the tribe leaders worried that the entire people would be destroyed. So they devised a plan.

With the help of cunning animals, the tribespeople dug seven pits high in the alpine meadows of the mountain range. They filled each hole with boiling, red liquid, then darted away to hide behind the old-growth firs.

One by one, each of the monsters lumbered through the lush valley and tripped headlong into a hole that the tribespeople had dug. The giants roared in agony, thrashing and splashing the lava over the sides of the pits, where it coursed across the landscape "as far as man can travel in a day." The monsters, entombed in the earth, stood in their holes forever, rising above the valley on display for all passersby to see, "to remind people that punishment comes from wrongdoing."

Keep that in mind, should you venture into the Hells Canyon Wilderness, where splendid monsters tower from the earth.

DO IT

For the best taste of the Hells Canyon Wilderness's alpine zones, hop on the Seven Devils Loop, a 26.7-mile marathon that circumnavigates the granite ramparts on Trails 101 and 124. From the Windy Saddle trailhead (45.349473, -116.512365), do it clockwise, spending nights at Dog Creek (near mile 8) and Baldy Lake (mile 19, via a short spur). If you're strapped for time, turn around at the Cannon Lakes. Depending on how far you venture up the valley, it's a 5- to 6-mile out-and-back to the twin tarns, which are cradled below Tower of Babel, She Devil, The Ogre, and The Goblin.

The Lost City

Cliff Palace, Cliff Palace Tour, Mesa Verde National Park, Colorado

O N THE morning of December 18, 1888, Richard Wetherill awoke to a blanket of white cloaking the red waves of the Colorado Plateau. The pinyons and junipers peeked out from the snow like they weren't sure, and the rancher broke down his camp and mounted a horse for the day's work: combing the cuesta for stray cattle.

Wetherill was familiar with the Four Corners and knew how to swiftly move across the untamed Mesa Verde, negotiating canyons, open desert, woodlands—and ruins. He and his family had happened upon archaeological sites themselves in the years prior and were aware that ancient sites had been discovered in the vicinity. But that wasn't on Wetherill's mind when, chasing down lost cattle, he landed at the doorstep of Cliff Palace, a city hewn of sandstone, nestled in the recesses beneath a vast overhang.

Cliff Palace, at one time more than 1,000 years ago, contained some 150 rooms and more than twenty kivas, or churchlike chambers. It's believed it housed more than a hundred Anasazi people—more than any other archaeological site protected in Mesa Verde National Park. As Wetherill later put it, Cliff Palace has all the appearances of a mirage.

Wetherill and two others—a fellow cowboy and a Ute guide—hastily clambered down from the sandstone ledge and entered the lost city. They were immediately taken with the elaborate stylings, the careful construction, and the clear picture of what life was like at one time. Water jugs and bowls sat undisturbed on tables, tools like axes rested on shelves, and children's toys lay scattered on the floor. It in no way looked as though Cliff Palace had been abandoned for the 600 years prior. In fact, it was quite the opposite: It looked like its residents would be returning at any minute, as though they'd simply walk through the opening in the sandstone after running an errand.

Even today, archaeologists can't agree why the Ancestral Puebloans left Mesa Verde, but the mirage sentiment is consistent. Visitors dating back more than 100 years have reported a spiritual power hanging there, while many others have noted feeling odd sensations and a heaviness to the air. Even the Ute guide who originally happened upon Cliff Palace with Wetherill once warned his boss, allegedly, that he should take care to preserve the site and not disturb spirits of the dead, or else, "you'll die, too."

DO IT

To see the Cliff Palace as Richard Wetherill did, take the guided tour of the same name. It only covers a quarter of a mile in distance, but it offers the most in-depth look at the cliff dwelling (nps. gov/meve). It starts from the Cliff Palace Overlook (37.167768, -108.473108). For a self-guided tour, check out the Spruce Tree House (Wetherill was believed to be the first white man to discover this dwelling, too), arguably the best-preserved site in the park. Start your exploration from the Chapin Mesa Archaeological Museum (37.183990, -108.489203). Lastly, while Mesa Verde may have been designated a national park to "preserve the works of man," its landscape itself is park-worthy: After visiting the archaeological sites, head east to the Morefield Campground, where you can tackle the 7.8-mile Prater Ridge Loop or the 2-mile Knife Edge out-and-back, both of which offer big views over the Colorado Plateau.

The Odyssey

Heart Lake, Heart Lake Trail,
Yellowstone National Park, Wyoming

TRUMAN EVERTS could not fall asleep. He lay on a bed of pine needles amid a thicket of trees, staring skyward at the blackness of the night, his ears perking every so often at the sounds of a barking coyote or a howling gray wolf. When a gust whipped through the grove, sending a shiver down his spine and dusting the earth with flurries, Everts clutched his empty stomach and started to think the worst. He was alone, lost, and inching closer to death.

Nearly a month prior, Everts and a small party had set out into Yellowstone country to explore and map what would soon become the first national park. At fifty-four, he was the oldest member of the company, and, for all intents and purposes, the least capable. He was a Vermont man who had most recently been slinging tax dollars behind a desk as the Assessor of Internal Revenue for the Montana Territory. Accepting a position in the Washburn Expedition seemed almost random, but calamity didn't ensue right away.

For a few weeks, the men had followed the Yellowstone River, detailing the snow-capped peaks, surging waterfalls, and geothermal features that characterize the park we know today. Apparently it wasn't unusual for members of the party—or at least Everts, who was conspicuously nearsighted—to be momentarily separated from the group in negotiating windfall, thick underbrush, and various other hazards, so the explorer wasn't concerned when he spun around in a dense pine grove to discover he was all alone. Instead, he picketed his horse, started a fire, found a plush bed of pine needles, and fell asleep, confident he'd rejoin the expedition in the morning.

The following day, however, Everts didn't link up with his group. He set out toward a peninsula on Yellowstone Lake where he supposed the men would be camping, but in navigating the dense woods on foot, he lost track of his horse. It could have been merely a minor setback if not for the fact that Everts's blankets, firearms, fishing tackle, matches, and food were packed in the mare's saddlebags. The bureaucrat was abandoned in the heart of the unforgiving Yellowstone backcountry with nothing but the clothes on his back and a pair of opera glasses.

The rogue explorer wandered through the woods in search of the expedition for four or five days, eating thistle roots and notably evading a mountain lion before the snowstorm blew in. He curled up beneath a large spruce tree and suffered through the longest night of his life. Everts awoke—or came to—the following morning understandably disappointed in his predicament. He endured another day in the shelter of the spruce boughs before making his way to a collection of natural hot springs and geothermal vents, where he spent a week huddled in their warmth. But his bad luck would continue there, too: The malnourished man rolled over into one of the cauldrons during his sleep one night, severely scalding his lower half.

Driven mad by hunger and pain, Everts's written records of his time in the Yellowstone backcountry are difficult to decipher, but he likely spent some two weeks bumbling in and around Yellowstone Lake before he claimed to have encountered a ghost.

"Go back immediately, as rapidly as your strength will permit," the apparition commanded Everts. "There is no food here, and the idea of scaling these rocks is madness."[15]

"[But] the distance is too great—I cannot live to travel it," Everts contended.

"Say not so," the ghost retorted. "Your life depends upon the effort! Return at once. Start now, lest your resolution falter. Travel as fast and as far as possible—it is your only chance."

And with that, the lost explorer resolved to make the odyssey of some 100 miles back along the Yellowstone River to where the expedition had set out. He moved slowly and only staved off death under the pretense that he now had a "traveling companion" in the ghost. When a grizzled mountain man discovered the gaunt Everts crawling along the forest floor thirty-seven days after he'd been separated from his expedition party, he was a mere fifty pounds, with feet worn to the bones and flesh wounds festering yellow.

Everts owed his salvation to the ghost, a "gift from the throne of the Eternal," and, for what it's worth, lived to more than eighty-four years of age, apparently no worse for the wear.

DO IT

It's believed that Truman Everts lost his company somewhere near Heart Lake—so that's where you should venture (but bring a map, of course). Begin at the Heart Lake trailhead (44.317347, -110.598335) and head 8 miles east past hot springs and meadows to the shore of one of Yellowstone's largest tarns. Reserve a campsite on the western banks, then retrace your steps on the return. Be sure to check out the Grand Canyon of the Yellowstone before leaving the park; the classic landmark was a highlight of the Washburn Expedition. (Good bet: Take the South Rim Trail 4.4 miles out and back from the Wapiti Lake trailhead.)

The Warrior Princess

Running Eagle Falls, Running Eagle Falls Trail, Glacier National Park, Montana

L ONG BEFORE Katniss, there was Running Eagle. She was a fierce warrior and a strategic mastermind and, yes, a woman. But before all of that, she was just a little girl who used to play amid the crinkle-cut peaks and cirque-cradled lakes that fall off the Continental Divide in northern Montana. At that time, she was called Pitamakan.

Pitamakan, a member of the Piegan tribe of the Blackfeet, was, for all intents and purposes, a tomboy. As the eldest of five, she had to learn from her mother how to raise a family and serve the domestic duties expected of women in the tribe, but whenever time allowed, she was exploring the woods. She loved to retreat to a unique waterfall she'd found because, like her, there was more to it than met the eye: Behind the 40-foot-tall curtain of whitewater, a smaller, 15-foot plume gushed from an opening in the brown rock wall. It was a double waterfall, a cascade with two identities, even though only one is visible from the outside.

Pitamakan's father, a well-respected warrior in the tribe, took notice of his daughter's love for the land and began teaching her the art of archery. She quickly picked up the skill, and when she was adept enough, her father invited her to tag along on the bison hunts. Many of the other warriors disapproved of a young girl joining the expeditions, but Pitamakan's father was important enough to not be questioned. And it was for the best: On one hunt, a group of warriors from an enemy tribe ambushed the Piegans. Legend has it that Pitamakan's father was shot from his horse, and his daughter, fifteen years old at the time, ran into enemy fire to rescue him. She heaved him onto her horse and sped away, evading harm and saving her father's life.

That alone would make for a great enough story, but Pitamakan's doesn't end there. Soon after the ambush, each of her parents died. Her father was killed in battle with the Crows and, it's said, her mother died of a broken heart. And so, before long, Pitamakan was the head of the household, as her mother had trained her. But, despite what she'd learned, the role never suited her. A few years later, she hired an old widow to care for and feed her siblings, like a housewife, and Pitamakan assumed the role of the man.

As expected, most of the tribespeople disapproved, but Pitamakan didn't care. She had always understood her identity as a warrior and a huntress, and that was magnified now, as she was fueled by rage and hurt. So one day, with her father's rifle lashed across her back, Pitamakan headed out to join the Piegan warriors on a mission to retrieve horses that had been stolen in a battle with the Crows. The war party argued with her, and the chief even refused to lead the mission if she tagged along, but Pitamakan's stubbornness won out when the medicine man announced that he felt strongly that she would bring the Blackfeet luck.

To prove her bravery, Pitamakan volunteered to sneak into the Crow camp first, as a scout. Her tribe consented, and so the girl, now twenty, crept along a river of swiftwater, ducking between conifers and boulders, and stealthily negotiating the toothy terrain until she happened upon the camp along the banks of Flathead Lake. There, she found their stable of horses and quietly freed those that belonged to her tribe before untethering some of the Crows' finest stallions. In all, Pitamakan snuck out of the camp on her scouting mission with eleven horses. When she returned to the Piegans, she was celebrated and congratulated—and given the name Running Eagle, allegedly the first woman to ever receive such recognition.

And yet, even with such an honorable name and a quickly growing résumé, Pitamakan couldn't shake others' views of her inherent weaknesses as a female. Even the tribal leaders weren't convinced, and they commanded her to go on a so-called spirit quest. Pitamakan was to leave the tribe for four days to fast and meditate and seek council from the Great Spirit. And so, as she had for her entire childhood, Pitamakan escaped to her waterfall. She climbed into the hidden grotto behind the water, a cave you can't see during the spring runoff, and received a vision alerting her to her true identity: Running Eagle.

When she returned, the chief elders no longer questioned her, assigning her to various expeditions and war parties for the rest of her life. Running Eagle even became a war chief before she was killed in battle near the age of thirty. She was treated as a hero and was well respected in the community—though she may never have left this earth for good. Piegan history suggests that tribespeople continued to see Running Eagle in the mist of the double waterfall that she frequently visited and viewed the spot as sacred. Even today, hikers have claimed to feel an otherworldly power or heaviness when they visit the falls where Pitamakan received her vision.

DO IT

Running Eagle's namesake falls sit between Lower Two Medicine Reservoir and Two Medicine Lake in East Glacier and are accessed via a super-easy, 0.6-mile loop from the trailhead by the same name (48.496129, -113.348458). You must time it for spring runoff if you want to see the 40-footer spilling over the top; any other time of year, Running Eagle Falls will comprise just the 15-footer that plunges out of the rock wall. Make it longer by tacking on a longer hike that crosses Pitamakan Pass and drops into the Pitamakan Lake basin to pay the warrior princess your full respect. (And this is Glacier National Park; more is always better.) To do that, keep driving west on Two Medicine Road from the Running Eagle Falls trailhead and park at the Two Medicine Campground (48.492150, -113.365451). From there, you can hike 8 or so miles to Pitamakan Lake by way of the Pitamakan Pass Trail, or you can tick off an instant classic: the 18-mile Dawson Pitamakan Loop.

A Bad Omen

North Platte River, Castle Trail, Guernsey State Park, Wyoming

I F SOMETHING happens once, it's random. Twice is interesting. Three times makes a pattern—which means it's worth keeping vigil for the Ship of Death when you're near the North Platte River.

It made its grand entrance into history in the mid-1800s, when a trapper named Leon Weber was tracking game along the North Platte near present-day Guernsey. There, the river, which courses more than 700 miles from the oxygen-starved peaks of Colorado's Rocky Mountains to the vast plains of Nebraska, twists its way through horseshoe bend after horseshoe bend. So it was odd, then, when Weber allegedly spotted a frigate adorned with huge white sails and a medley of cannons cutting through the mist on the water. A chill ran down his spine as he stopped to watch. The crewmembers were crowded on the deck, but, in unison, they stepped back to reveal a limp corpse sprawled across the wood. Weber wasn't sure, but it looked as though it was the fragile body of his fiancée, slain. Bewildered, he did a double-take, but when he peeked back at the North Platte, there was nothing there, just the swift blue water.

Thinking he was going mad, Weber saddled up and headed home to rest. But when he arrived, he learned his fiancée had died earlier that day.

A few decades passed before a rancher named Gene Wilson, who was driving a herd of cattle near the North Platte, stopped dead in his tracks. An unusually thick fog head seemed to be slowly moving upstream, like a bulldozer. And then, odder still, a huge warship seemed to materialize out of the mist, taking form in the middle of the river. The confused cattleman peered out to the brigantine where he spied what appeared to be his wife, dead and sprawled across the deck. The terrified Wilson sped home only to learn that his dear wife had passed away that day.

In fifteen years it happened again, this time to poor Victor Heibe, a soft-spoken man who was outside of his waterfront farmstead pruning a tree. The man saw what he believed was a massive frigate taking form amid a thick cloud on the water—and then what looked like the body of his friend. As with Weber and Wilson, Heibe soon learned that the friend he'd seen on the ghost ship died later that day.

Thankfully, the Ship of Death hasn't preluded any deaths in the past century—but we still recommend averting your eyes if the fog rolls in when you're on the river.

DO IT

String together any of the trails in Guernsey State Park and you're guaranteed views over the free-flowing North Platte or the reservoir where it's been dammed. Many of the paths are paved or suitable for mountain biking, but there's a nice hiker-only path that begins near the turnaround on Castle Drive (42.321041, -104.783298). From there, you can trace the bluffs that frame the reservoir west or east as far as you'd like before retracing your steps.

Spirit Lake

Grand Lake, East Inlet Trail,
Rocky Mountain National Park, Colorado

"G RAND" SEEMS a fitting name for the state's largest and deepest lake, but perhaps its first moniker was even better. Long ago, it's said, a herd of bison lumbered down from the alpine meadows cradled along the Continental Divide. It was winter, and the lake, the headwaters of the mighty Colorado River, was frozen. The bison roamed across the 1.5-mile-long lake, leaving trails of prints in the soft snow.

Meanwhile, a fisherman walked out onto the surface to find an opening through which to cast a line when he noticed a gaping hole in the sheet of ice. Massive, frying pan-size hoofprints seemed to lead out of the maw, so the curious fisherman tracked them to where they ended: back at the hole in the ice. He concluded that a spirit bison lived beneath the surface and people began calling the tarn accordingly: Spirit Lake.

Years later, the Utes, who thrived on the western side of the divide, were camped on the banks of Spirit Lake. One day, a famous Colorado summertime thunderhead rolled over the Never Summer Mountains to the north, turning the sky an eerie shade of green. As the tribespeople busied themselves making preparations for the deluge that was sure to come, a swarm of warriors from the Cheyenne and Arapaho tribes stormed through the woods that trim Spirit Lake, raining arrows through the camp. The Utes, knowing they were both outnumbered and unprepared, had no choice but to send all of their women and children into the lake on a raft. The refugees drifted through the water, safe from the war, but not the thunderstorm.

The battle raged through the night before the Cheyenne and Arapaho fled back over the divide. When the Ute chief scanned the lake, however, all he saw were the timber remains of the raft, bobbing in the slate water in the pale lavender light of morning. Every single woman and child had drowned in Spirit Lake. The Utes supposedly watched the ghosts of their dearly departed rise out of the water like swirling mists and vowed to move what remained of their tribe away from the clutches of the haunted tarn. The Utes had all but disappeared from the area by the late 1870s.

The women and children of the Ute tribe wouldn't be the last to die in Spirit Lake, but they're perhaps the most noteworthy. Some locals still claim to see the outline of those who perished floating in the mist that often hangs over the lake in the morning. Come wintertime, when Grand Lake freezes over, people have claimed to hear the piercing cries of women and children trapped beneath the ice.

Grand in scope, sure, but grander in spirit.

DO IT

The eponymous lake is in the small mountain hamlet, Grand Lake, near the west entrance into Rocky Mountain National Park. (Convenient, huh?) There are a number of trails around the lake (Shadow Mountain Trail is the best for views of the lake), but you'd be remiss to skip out on the national park when you're already this close, so head out on the East Inlet Trail, which begins from, you guessed it, Grand Lake's east inlet (40.239615, -105.799942). Take it roughly 8 miles to Spirit Lake, a small alpine pool that was essentially regifted Grand Lake's original name, before retracing your steps to the trailhead. Reserve a campsite along the way; numbers 61 to 68 are en route (the higher numbers are farther east toward Spirit Lake and the Continental Divide).

The Frenchwoman

MacDonald Pass, Continental Divide Trail, Helena National Forest, Montana

THE YOUNG farmhand smelled it before he saw it, the metallic odor wafting through the open door and tickling his nostrils. He dismounted his horse and peered through the doorway into the rustic suite. And there, beneath an arch made of logs and between a bed of burgundy linens and a mahogany table set for two was the proprietor's wife, a thirty-something beauty with jet-black hair, lying face down in a pool of her own blood.

The woman, Madame Guyot she was called, operated the nearby toll road for her husband. He had built the dirt path over 6,312-foot Mac-Donald Pass in the mid-1860s to make travel easier between Helena and Deer Lodge Valley (the young Montana Territory lacked the money to do it internally), and the madame collected the tolls. In the evenings, she played hostess at the nearby hostel where passing travelers could land a room and a meal for $3. Men lauded Madame Guyot's hospitality, often stopping prematurely or pressing on into the night for the sole purpose of paying a visit to the Frenchwoman's cabin. On any given night, as many as thirty itinerants could be found packed into the dorm room, spilling out of beds and sprawled on the floor.

But Madame Guyot had at least two secrets. The first was that her husband, the wealthy French-Canadian Constant Guyot, was an abusive drunkard. He'd spend his days working a hay field a few miles from the toll road, then come back to the cabin to hit the bottle—and his wife. The second was that she was slowly pocketing money the duo earned. She'd take some of every toll or room fare to the extent that more than $6,000 worth of gold was allegedly stolen from her quarters the day she was murdered.

Old periodicals suggest that Madame Guyot had plans to siphon off enough gold to leave the wild sagebrush plains and pine woods for France sometime in the following fall, but fate and a cold-blooded killer bonded her to west-central Montana. In the years that followed her unsolved murder, the Frenchwoman was spotted lurking amid the lodgepoles near the pass along the Continental Divide and among the low-hanging timber beams in the old cabin. Later, travelers began reporting picking up a mysterious female hitchhiker, only to peer into the rearview mirror to see that she had completely disappeared. Their descriptions varied, but they always included the fact that the woman had jet-black hair.

DO IT

The 3,100-mile Continental Divide Trail intersects MacDonald Pass, so pay a visit to the Frenchwoman's Road and knock off a section of the long path. (The cabin is no longer standing, but it was west off the pass, near Dog Creek.) In theory, you could go as far as Canada, but weekend warriors may prefer to head 6 miles north from the trailhead off US 12 (46.561344, -112.308723) through a canopy of lodgepole pines and past old mines to Priest Pass. Or, keep going another 4 or 5 miles beyond that to camp on the slopes of 7,505-foot Greenhorn Mountain. Conversely, you could always go south. No matter which way you go, beware the hitchhikers.

Beat a Dead Horse

Star Dune, Great Sand Dunes,
Great Sand Dunes National Park, Colorado

L ADY DIED when she was three. It wasn't a natural death, which is unsurprising given that most Appaloosas live well into their twenties. But what was surprising was that it was decidedly unnatural: The mare, who had spent her days prancing and cavorting around a ranch at the base of 14,244-foot Blanca Peak in Colorado's photogenic Sangre de Cristo Range, was found the morning of September 9, 1967, with no flesh on her head or neck. Weirder still, the slice where the fur ended above her shoulders was perfectly straight and smooth, with no signs of gore, as though it had been cauterized. In fact, there was no blood around the horse at all.

As the media bore into the case, more and more oddities popped up. The carcass, for example, smelled strongly of chemicals. When a forestry aide used a Geiger counter to measure radioactivity in the area, the reading was off the charts. There were half a dozen inexplicable circular indentations in the brush north of where the corpse had been found and black exhaust smudges to the southeast. Lady's owner, Nellie Lewis, mentioned that she had found a tool she didn't recognize near the mare's body; when she picked it up, it burned her skin. Some people suggested that the horse had died of an infection and scavengers had picked it—parts of it, anyway—clean. Some suggested that a motley crew of rowdy teens was to blame. But neither explanation accounted for all of the peculiarities—and neither sat well with Lewis.

Taking matters into her own hands, Lewis sent for her Lady to be autopsied. The pathology results were unbelievable: Lady's brain, chest, and abdominal cavities were completely emptied of organs, and her

spinal column had been drained of fluid. After this piece of news filtered through the wires, the theorists had a whale of a time: Lady had been struck by lightning; Lady had been held by her hind legs and dunked into acid, whereupon the jokesters pulled her organs out, individually, through her mouth; Lady had fallen ill and died near a random, flesh-eating colony of ants, which had previously wandered through radioactive sand; and, maybe the least unreasonable of them all, that Lady had been the unlucky subject of an alien experiment.

Before you take a guess, though, you should know that there have been more reported UFO sightings in the San Luis Valley than anywhere else in the world.

DO IT

Alien abduction will seem a worthwhile risk when you first catch a glimpse of the country's biggest sandbox nestled beneath a wall of snow-capped Fourteeners. The best way to do it is as an overnight (also easier to spy UFOs at nighttime; win-win). From the Dunes Parking Lot (37.739668, -105.517159), start walking and camp wherever the urge strikes beyond 1.5 miles. There are no trails and no designated campsites. Star Dune, the continent's tallest dune at 750 feet, will get you closest to the sky; target it near 37.751484, -105.558197, about 1.5 very slow miles from the parking lot.

Little People Eaters

Owyhee Canyonlands, Corral Canyon, North Fork Owyhee Wilderness, Idaho

THE HUNTER moved deftly across the shrubby steppe on a still morning. He was tall with dark skin, colored a deep copper by the sun, and carried a bow. The day was beginning to overtake the dusk as the man ducked into a steep-sided, mahogany-and-black canyon on the prowl for bighorn sheep. Hugging the canyon wall, he galloped up and over volcanic-rock benches and through a skinny slot. But he hesitated on a ledge that jutted out over the chasm that splits present-day southwestern Idaho. Ahead, curling out of the canyon's innards, was a narrow plume of smoke.

It was odd: No one lived in this canyon, and it was far too remote and rugged for the man to expect company. And that's, for the most part, as it remains today. The 4,500-square-mile Owyhee Canyonlands, which span multiple wilderness areas and cross into Oregon, are some of the country's remotest terrain outside Alaska. You'd be more likely to encounter a mule deer or pronghorn than another human.

And so, curious, the hunter pursued the black ribbon that twisted and faded into the dusk. It led him to a small home hewn from rock and tucked in a corner of the canyon. He stopped outside the dwelling and heard a voice say, "Someone is here. Someone wants to come in." The brave hunter stepped inside the shelter and was taken aback: In front of him stood a small creature, no more than 3 feet tall with a long, coiled tail. The monster had human-like features—eyes, a nose, and ears—but his skin was tough and brown, like that of an elephant. The hunter had heard stories of his tribespeople encountering these creatures in the rocky gashes that snaked through the high desert, though no one who had been trapped by one had ever returned: It was widely known that the dwarves were cannibals.

"You are a good person to bring yourself to me so I can eat you," the dwarf cooed.

"Yes," the man quickly replied. "I'll wait while you prepare a delicious meal."

The dwarf consented and turned its back to arrange spices, allowing the hunter a spare moment to devise a strategy. He spun around, looking for an opening through which to escape, and, in doing so, he noticed half a dozen hearts lashed to the wall. "Whose hearts line your shelter?" he asked the dwarf, his mind reeling.

"Those are my family's," the monster replied. "One belongs to my father, and one my mother, and the others my siblings. That one behind you is mine," it finished.

Without pause, the hunter grabbed an arrow from his satchel and stabbed the heart behind him. The creature dropped to the ground before him and died immediately. Knowing the dwarf's family would soon be returning from their hunts, the man walked the perimeter of the inside of the rock hut, piercing each heart one by one. When he was done, he sprinted from the hidden shelter and returned to his village, where he was regarded as a hero for defeating the cannibal dwarves.

But the story doesn't end there. It's believed that there's an entire race of these evil dwarves, so while the hunter evaded and killed some half a dozen, an entire population still lurks in the shadows of rocky places from the Great Plains west toward the coast. Multiple Native American tribes believed in and told stories about these cannibal dwarves, and while the details differ, the general consensus is that they prefer remote, rugged, and seldom-visited landscapes—not unlike the Owyhee Canyonlands.

DO IT

Very few official trails snake through the North Fork Owyhee and Owyhee River Wildernesses, which means you must be an advanced navigator—and if you happen on a footpath, it's most likely been forged by hikers, game, or dwarves. Easiest option: Set up a base camp at the North Fork Recreation Site (42.593377, -116.981431) and stage simple day hikes to explore the canyon and Sahara-like high desert from the car campground. Adventurer's option: Make a 16-mile loop out of Corral Canyon. Start from where Mud Flat Road turns into Juniper Mountain Road (42.572543, -116.735702), and head north into narrow Corral Canyon. Follow the path of least resistance along the creek to camp some 8 miles north (find a shaded spot with easy water access, preferably established). Next day, loop back along the Current Creek, again following the path of least resistance. There are tight slots in the canyon; scan for monsters there.

Southwest

Crash Canyon

Chuar and Temple Buttes, Beamer Trail,
Grand Canyon National Park, Arizona

"SALT LAKE, United 718," came in a garbled, unidentified radio transmission on June 30, 1956. "Ah! We're going in!" Moments earlier, United Airlines Flight 718, a Chicago-bound passenger flight, cut through the clouds and collided with another jet airliner, slicing through the latter's fuselage. The skewered plane nosed over, plummeting into the Grand Canyon, 21,000 feet below. Seats, luggage, and people were sucked out of the open cabin as the plane, TWA Flight 2, spun to the canyon floor in a fiery wreckage.

United Airlines Flight 718 had lost an engine and part of its left wing as the pilot fought to keep it out of the canyon's maw. But a minute later, the commander had lost control, radioing one final message as the aircraft hurtled into the Big Ditch. It crashed into a redrock tower, obliterating all passengers. At the time, it was the worst commercial airline disaster in history, stealing 128 lives, passengers and crew, among the two craft and ultimately sparking the creation of the Federal Aviation Administration.

It took a team of military personnel, Swiss mountaineers, and American recreationists—rock climbers, river guides, and hikers—to locate the wreckage. Deep in the remote corner of Grand Canyon National Park, between Temple and Chuar Buttes, just south of the confluence of the Colorado and Little Colorado Rivers, the search teams found wing panels, chunks of fuselage, propeller pieces, and unidentifiable human remains. Fewer than thirty of the 128 deceased were positively identified.

And while the passengers of each plane are memorialized—United Airlines Flight 718 at Grand Canyon Cemetery and TWA Flight 2 at

Citizens Cemetery in Flagstaff—some hikers suspect that their spirits remain in the canyon. Campers have reported seeing unattached lights, as though a group of people was hiking single file out of the canyon, only to discover no one actually there. Some have reported seeing the lights on the west side of the river—which you can't even access on foot—where the debris of the plane collision was found. In one tale, a ranger claimed to have seen a dozen or so people dressed in city clothes hiking out of the canyon from the ravine between Temple and Chuar Buttes. But when she crawled out of her tent to investigate, the people were nowhere to be seen.

DO IT

There's only one way to steal a view of the crash site, and it's for experts only: Connect the Tanner and Beamer Trails 18.5 miles to the Little Colorado River (navigation prowess required). It's about 6.7 miles (descending some 4,600 feet) to the Colorado River from Lipan Point (36.032662, -111.852436). Pick a beachside campsite (permit pending) before continuing north along the Colorado about 3 miles to another beach campsite beside Palisades Creek on the Beamer Trail. Leave camp the next morning on a day mission: Keep going north on the Beamer Trail about 4 miles to a viewpoint of Crash Canyon. Look west across the Colorado to the natural gash between Temple and Chuar Buttes. Turn around here or continue about 2 miles to the confluence of the Colorado and Little Colorado Rivers to break by the 100-year-old Beamer Cabin before retracing your steps to camp. From there, climb out of the canyon by the same route you descended.

Bloodsucker

Southeast Texas, Turkey Creek Trail, Big Thicket National Preserve, Texas

INCLUDING JUST a single hike relating to the notorious Chupacabra in this book seems unfair. After all, the legendary bloodsucker is famously linked to a region that spans more than 3,000 miles. But somewhere in the midst of that area is one spot where the Chupacabra almost seems a natural fit.

Deep in the southeast corner of Texas, worlds collide in Big Thicket National Preserve. Longleaf pine forests abut cypress-lined bayous, and dark, murky swamps border sun-blasted deserts. It's an ecological wonderland that plays host to A-list fauna, like black bears, mountain lions, bobcats, foxes, river otters, and armadillos. That's, of course, what they'll put in the brochure, but the list of wildlife doesn't end there. Big Thicket is home to alligators, mosquitoes, ticks, chiggers, at least eleven species of bats, four species of venomous snakes, and the list goes on. Chupacabra would be in good company—and it's been spotted nearby, too, so not out of the question.

The rise of Chupacabra (literally "goat sucker") dates back to the mid-1990s, when a Puerto Rican farmer discovered eight of his sheep had been mysteriously killed. They had appeared perfectly intact, almost as though they were simply taking midday siestas on the grassy slope, but a closer inspection revealed that each ewe suffered puncture wounds. Someone or something had drained the livestock of their blood. The story gained traction, and more and more people reported odd attacks of a similar nature in Central and South America. The number of incidents in Puerto Rico alone topped 200. People described a bipedal creature, about 3 feet tall, with short, gray fur and spikes coming out of its back.

A decade later, however, Chupacabra had migrated north to the States. Alleged sightings occurred all over the country, but if someone was to draw up a heat map, the highest concentration of red would be in south-southeast Texas, near Big Thicket. Chupacabra retained most of its original identity from the 90s with a few changes: It was reported as an almost canine-like monster that stalked livestock on all fours and, in lieu of matted gray fur, it had rough, gray skin.

Add it to the list.

DO IT

The best way to ensure more wildlife (and monster) sightings is to spend more time out there: Do Big Thicket on a 15-mile, point-to-point overnight on the Turkey Creek Trail. From the parking lot on Farm to Market Road (30.613462, -94.344337), work your way south along the trail's namesake. Find an at-large campsite (between miles 9 and 10), and exit at the Kirby Nature Center (30.462480, -94.350148). Consider caching water on Gore Store Road beforehand, and beware the wildlife and carnivorous plants, in addition to Chupacabras. You can also pick a piece of this trip to do as a day hike.

The Escape Artist

Davis Gulch, Davis Gulch Trail, Grand Staircase-Escalante National Monument, Utah

God, how the trail lures me. You cannot comprehend its resistless fascination for me. . . I'll never stop wandering. And when the time comes to die, I'll find the wildest, loneliest, most desolate spot there is.
— Everett Ruess, July 12, 1933

YOU CAN find lonely corners of desert solitude throughout the Southwest, but there are none more remote than the redrock chasms, snaking slots, and watery oases of the 1.9-million-acre Grand Staircase-Escalante National Monument. Just to reach an access point, you must manage your way to south-central Utah, the closest "major" city being more than a five-hour drive away. Then from Escalante, Utah (population: 783), it's more than 50 miles southeast down a relentlessly bumpy, unpaved washboard road to the best trailheads.

But once you're there, it's the sort of landscape that hikers' dreams are made of, a sprawling fantasyland of sandstone buttes, slickrock waves, narrow chutes, and never-ending canyons. And imagine, that's not even the half of it—literally. In 1963, the final bucket of concrete was poured on the Glen Canyon Dam, effectively sealing the Colorado River near Page, Arizona. The rising water of Lake Powell submerged Glen Canyon, and, within a decade, many of its sinuous side canyons, including those bored by the Escalante.

The area may have avoided certain fate if its biggest cheerleader was around to campaign for it, but the fact remains, no one knows what happened to Everett Ruess. The enigmatic Ruess left his parents' Los Angeles home in 1931 to explore the West. He was an artist and a poet, and while on his travels, the teenager frequently wrote letters home, the best means we have for tracking his route and exploits. He was small in stature with sandy-colored hair and looked, for all intents and purposes, like a kid, but Ruess was exceedingly precocious.

He traveled through the Sierra and across the Colorado Plateau, humming operas and symphonies and supposedly paying his way with watercolor paintings. He allegedly learned the Navajo language and spent time with Mormon pioneers; he studied with archaeologists and partook in Hopi ceremonies. He created a reputation for himself that would solidify him as a sort of folk hero among outdoors enthusiasts 70 years later, but after three years exploring the American West, he was ready, it seems, to settle down. And it was the Escalante that he returned to.

In November 1934, the twenty-year-old Ruess rode into the small town of Escalante with two burros, one of which was carrying a load of camping gear. "As to when I shall visit civilization, it will not be soon, I think," he wrote in what would be his final letter to his family. "I prefer the saddle to the street-car, the star-sprinkled sky to a roof." Ruess posted the letter and then ventured south into the fissures of Escalante, where he built a small camp and a corral. He etched his pseudonym, Nemo (Latin for "nobody"), into the desert varnish on the rock face and was never seen again.

DO IT

Do not go the way of Everett Ruess; expert navigators only. From an unnamed trailhead off Hole-in-the-Rock Road (37.257549, -110.986198), navigate across open slickrock and past sandstone domes on a barely-there stock trail, paralleling the tentacle of Davis Gulch. Roughly 5 miles in, the path descends steeply into the chasm at the last-known camp of Ruess. Depending on water levels, you can venture northeast through the narrows toward Lake Powell, passing arches, waterfalls, and petroglyphs. (The "Nemo" etching is now underwater.) Otherwise, spin around and head roughly 2 miles southwest through the canyon to visit Ruess's horse corral (37.298870, -110.953102) and locomotive-size Bement Arch (37.283791, -110.964798). Retrace your steps roughly 7 miles to the trailhead.

Vanishing Act

Chaco Canyon, Peñasco Blanco Trail,
Chaco Canyon National Historical Park,
New Mexico

T HE WIND whips through the high desert, sending tumbleweeds bouncing across the vast wash and kicking up a dust devil that whirls amid the sagebrush. It's barren, a wasteland, but there's hidden beauty here: When the dust settles, make out the outline of a curious elk watching you from the other side of the canyon or a claret cup cactus exploding with red blooms beneath a sandstone overhang. Or listen for baying coyotes piercing the stillness as the afternoon wanes. Or scan for the ruins of an ancient city.

More than 60 miles removed from the nearest town and a three-hour drive from Albuquerque, Chaco Canyon might seem an unusual place for a city center. But, 1,000 years ago, this desertscape was where you would have found American civilization's first power hub. It comprised more than thirteen different pueblos, or communities, housing thousands of early humans. Like Manhattan or Los Angeles, Chaco Canyon directed the power and trading of the Anasazi and, thus, the history of people—which makes it doubly eerie walking down the abandoned wash.

The air is heavy in Chaco Canyon, and visitors report feeling like they're stepping in a literal ghost town. Some have filed reports of actual ghost encounters, while others say they've felt suddenly inconsolable. True, more than 5,000 cliff dwellers thrived here at one point. See their city center and apartments, which are arranged in some sort of hierarchical pattern. Notice that the windows in their houses are arranged to face specific constellations or solstices—a nice touch, especially given that the

Anasazi didn't have modern tech equipment or even compasses. See their ancient roadways, which they used to walk—no wheels, yet—goods, like turquoise, to traders from other civilizations. Visit their places of worship, some of which they burned, presumably ceremoniously, before they left. Because, at some point, a fifty-year drought made life on the high desert nearly impossible.

Studies indicate that the Anasazi uprooted likely in or around the 1200s and headed north, traveling more than 100 miles on an exodus to the fertile Mesa Verde (read more in The Lost City chapter on page 138). From there, we know, the ancient peoples left again, but to where or for what reason, we don't. They simply vanished from the face of the earth.

DO IT

For the best sampler, take the 3.6-mile Peñasco Blanco Trail, which leads to the third-largest archaeological site in the park (and a panorama of Chaco Canyon). Short spurs to see the petroglyphs and pictographs should be considered mandatory. (Regarding the latter, there's a panel containing a crescent moon, star, and hand-print—called the Supernova—that's easily discernible from the trail. The mind reels.) Begin from the parking lot at Pueblo del Arroyo (36.062385, -107.965439) and parallel the wash north-west to the Peñasco Blanco ruins; with spurs, expect it to be an 8-mile out-and-back.

Fool's Gold

Weaver's Needle, Peralta Trail,
Superstition Wilderness, Arizona

J ACOB WALTZ was an ordinary man. Born in Germany in the early 1800s, he immigrated to the States toward the middle of the century seeking economic opportunity. He held a handful of odd jobs along the Atlantic seaboard, including some mining gigs in the Carolinas and Alabama that didn't amount to much. He slowly made his way west, supposedly working at a tannery and another mine in California. There was absolutely nothing remarkable about Jacob Waltz—except that he was the only person to know the whereabouts of the country's richest mine.

This much people agree on. There are tomes devoted to the varying threads from here, but perhaps what happened next was that Waltz traveled to Mexico with a buddy, Jacob Weiser. It's impossible to say why the two men headed south, but most sources suggest that it was nothing more than a good adventure, a couple of friends horsing around before returning to their responsibilities. At some point during their exploits, the men encountered a game of cards that had turned crooked. Waltz wasn't a particularly big man, but he had a sort of bravado about him and didn't think twice about standing up to the local thug who was cheating money. It became the original trivial detail of a much larger legend.

See, a Spanish Don by the name of Miguel Peralta was lurking somewhere in the dark recesses of the tavern. Impressed with the two Germans, he asked them if they'd work for him. Peralta said he managed a mine somewhere in the heart of the Superstition Mountains, and he wanted the two friends to provide protection for his crew when they were traveling through Apache territory. In return, he'd give them a cut of the mine's profits. Details were scant, but the friends weren't picky. They agreed.

Waltz and Weiser accompanied Peralta into the craggy heart of the Superstitions to somewhere within the shadow of Weaver's Needle, a distinct parapet that rises out of the toothy skyline. There, supposedly, they witnessed Peralta's guys hauling ore from the desert's innards by the drum.

It suited them for a while—scaring off Apaches and defending the mine from thieves—but the Germans eventually bought Peralta out. They gave him all of their earnings in return for sole ownership of the mine. In the time that followed, the men amassed a fortune, but the exact amount would be untold. Weiser was killed in an Apache raid, and, scared, Waltz camouflaged the mine and fled. Twenty years later, on his deathbed, he told his caretaker where it was hidden. She never found it, and years later her son was discovered with a shotgun blast to the skull.

In more than a century since, parties have searched far and wide for Waltz's mystery mine, but no one has located it. (People began calling it the "Lost Dutchman's Mine," which is probably a misinterpretation of "Deutsch.") Maps have gone missing, hard evidence misplaced. Treasure hunters venture into the diadem of ramparts forming the Superstitions with clear directions and bulletproof theories only to return empty-handed, or worse, never at all. It seems every few years hikers looking for the gold go missing.

For as ordinary as he was, Waltz kept an extraordinary secret.

DO IT

From the Peralta trailhead (33.397160, -111.347980), it's about 2.3 miles up the Peralta Trail to the Fremont Saddle, which, at around 3,800 feet of elevation, offers a bird's-eye vantage down Peralta Canyon and into East Boulder Canyon. Spy tooth-shaped, 4,553-foot Weaver's Needle to the north (and keep your eyes peeled for flickers of gold). Turn around here to make it a full day hike, or keep going, linking any number of trails, to create a meaty overnight. Fit hikers (with navigation chops) can manage a cross-country tour de force across the Superstitions from here, taking West Boulder and Old West Boulder Canyons west. You'll cross the top of the iconic Flatiron before coasting down Siphon Draw to the trailhead of the same name in Lost Dutchman State Park near mile 12.

Paranormal Activity

Rock Canyon, Rock Canyon Trail,
Uinta National Forest, Utah

I
T'S THE second look that unnerves people. One look could be your imagination playing tricks, wires misfiring in your brain. But it's the double-take, when you crane your neck and look up to the top of the crags and confirm what you've seen that triggers the fight-or-flight response. Because there, on the jagged massif, is a ghostly man with a jack-o'-lantern grin, and in a moment, he leaps.

So many firsthand accounts of paranormal experiences in Rock Canyon like this saturate hiker forums and logs that the consistency is almost as alarming as the notion itself. People describe family outings, casual walks, or climbing approaches through the open-book gully that ultimately end with a glimpse of a creepy, pale human gawking at them and then chasing them out of the canyon. They describe a figure who stands like a gargoyle on a rock ledge before diving headlong and racing down the sheer quartzite toward the onlooker.

But beyond that, beyond the anecdotes, there's little to go off of. Rock Canyon's unique geology—vertical faces of yellow-and-red quartzite and gray limestone—have made it a haven for climbers, both trad and sport, so some people suggest that it's the ghost of one who perished years ago. Others suggest that the haunt has something to do with a nineteenth-century feud between the Mormons and Utes that ultimately resulted in the death of a Native American woman (hence why Squaw Peak is so-named).

If this is enough to make you squirm, then we don't recommend exploring any of the caves or abandoned tunnels in the canyon, either. You may even want to refrain from Googling them, to be honest.

DO IT

Consider the 3.4-mile Rock Canyon Trail a jumping-off point for a bigger adventure. A main vein through the canyon, it services the best climbing areas and caves, and it connects with other trails. Link it with the Squaw Peak Trail to make a 7.3-mile out-and-back to the top of the 7,862-footer (begin at the parking lot at 40.264723, -111.630452). Keep your eyes peeled for mountain goats, rock climbers, and, well, you know.

The Renegade

Mouse's Tank, Mouse's Tank Trail,
Valley of Fire State Park, Nevada

I T'S SAID that Valley of Fire State Park earned its name because when dusk's low-angle sunshine hits the redrock just so, it looks like a blaze erupting across the Mojave. The kaleidoscopic color show is reason enough to visit, but between the flaming-red sandstone outcroppings, there's more. Intricate petroglyphs adorn the canyon walls and Seussian waves of stone seem to ebb and flow around the brittlebush. Natural arches provide window views and narrow slots creep into the heart of the desert. And, somewhere mingled with it all, is the legacy of one of the area's most polarizing figures.

Little Mouse was a young Southern Paiute man, likely in his early twenties by the time he starting disrupting the peace. In the late 1800s, there was a sort of tug-of-war battle going on between the whites and the Natives over land rights, and the Paiutes were losing traction. Mouse, at the time, was working a gig as a ferryman on the Colorado River, shuttling people back and forth across the then-free-flowing Colorado, colored electric-blue by lime sediment. He got into some trouble for stealing from a local outfitter and wreaking havoc on a mining camp after a night of drinking, but the law didn't really hang down on him until two prospectors were found murdered.

Details are fuzzy, but whether Mouse actually committed the crime or was wise to the fact that he'd be the obvious suspect, he left. With nothing but the clothes on his back and a small satchel, he set out into the Mojave Desert.

Padding through the grit, the midsummer sun baking his back and shoulders, the man likely pulled off into the redrock cathedral for no other reason than for a respite. He was brown from years in the sun, broadened from years of manual labor, and calloused from a life in the desert, but even Mouse could have appreciated the refuge. And there, between the folds of redrock, in the heart of the present-day park, the man somehow landed upon a natural depression that held months' worth of rainwater. He had everything he needed and no reason to believe any sheriff could track him through the unforgiving Mojave.

But every man has a breaking point. It's not known how long Mouse hid out in the Valley of Fire, drinking from his natural bathtub and harvesting roots and small game, but the man grew lonely. He climbed out of the maze and, at some point, ended up on the other side of the park where the old Muddy River used to flow south before joining the Virgin River. And there, the legend goes, Mouse was cornered near the banks of the water. When he refused to surrender, a posse of half a dozen gunmen lit him up, setting the backdrop of sandstone alight in the most brilliant shade of red.

DO IT

It's an easy, 0.8-mile out-and-back to the renegade's hideout via the Mouse's Tank Trail. From the Petroglyph Canyon trailhead off White Domes Road (36.441028, -114.516216), head east along a flat wash that's cut between steep walls of redrock (the observant can spy trail-side rock art). Turn around at the natural basin of water that sustained Mouse to complete the hike. Back at the trailhead, stay north on the main road to tick off the 1-mile Rainbow Vista Trail; time it for sunset when the day's last rays ignite the sandstone.

Wild, Wild West

South Rim, South Rim Trail,
Big Bend National Park, Texas

N ATIVES, COWBOYS, soldiers, good guys, bad guys—
they've all been killed here. Big Bend doesn't discriminate:
At least 219 homicides have occurred within what's now
the national park boundaries.

Perhaps the most famous is Chief Alsate, who still
watches over the land from the Chisos Mountains today. Scan to the red
cliffs of Pulliam Bluff and you'll see the profile of a reclining man, his
lips parted, as though in agony: Alsate, the last of the Chisos Apaches.
As the legend goes, a man by the name of Leonecio Castillo betrayed the
marauding Alsate to Mexican officials. Convicted, the chief was brutally
executed by a Mexican firing squad.

Before long, however, sheepherders and vaqueros began seeing the
murdered man inexplicably wandering the Chisos Mountains. In one
case, they spied him lingering by a cave amid the redrock. Mexican officials investigated, and they found a bed of grass, animal bones, and warm
ashes inside the rocky recesses—as though someone were hiding out. The
officials also identified moccasin tracks that led nowhere in the pink dust.
Word got out to Castillo, the traitor, and, petrified, he bolted.

One evening, when Castillo was in hiding, he lay on the ground, lost
in thought, watching the rising moon paint the peaks lavender. He chuck-
led to himself when he considered that he was actually frightened of a
dead man. The renegade Alsate could never avenge him. But as he looked
out to the Chisos, he saw the outline of the man he'd betrayed, plainly, and
he knew Alsate would haunt him for the rest of his days. What happened
next is up for debate, but Castillo was never seen again.

Alsate, though, lived on. He watches over the desert from the crumbly cliffs of the Chisos, and he may also be responsible for the unexplainable green lights that seem to float on West Texas's horizon (Google "Marfa lights"). Some say he's holding a lantern, searching for his betrayer in the night.

With some 218 other murders, there's no shortage of ghost stories. Look for the cloaked specter of a double-crossed Mexican man in Bruja (Spanish for "witch") Canyon; listen for the pleading cries of a young woman who drowned herself in the Rio Grande to defy her captors; or hear the wail of a mother who was forced to drop her infant over a cliff because he was believed to be half animal.

DO IT

You can see Alsate's profile in Pulliam Bluff from the north-south Basin Junction road, which cuts through Big Bend, or you can explore Maple Canyon on foot (maps indicate a trail, but plan to bushwhack). Find the trailhead off the Basin Junction road (29.292818, -103.273759). To truly explore the Chisos, try the 14-mile South Rim Loop: From the Chisos Mountain Lodge (29.270080, -103.301373), connect the Laguna Meadows, Southwest Rim, Boot Canyon, and Pinnacles Trails into a counterclockwise circuit. Camp on the rim and plan on packing in all water. Don't become the 220th.

The Hermit

Reavis Ranch, Reavis Ranch Trail,
Superstition Wilderness, Arizona

AUTHORITIES FOUND Elisha Reavis's body beneath a juniper tree overlooking a valley. Ironically, it was the sort of spot the man would have loved if he was alive: views down a canyon to the manzanita-dotted desert, in the shadow of a 6,000-foot peak, a crystal-clear spring flowing nearby. It's the side of Arizona that even locals don't often know about. And, on a pleasant May day, it would have been positively romantic. Reavis, however, laid in a bloody heap not more than a few steps from the trail. And 20 feet down the path was his head.

Four miles away, tucked amid a circle of craggy needles, was Reavis's home, an Eden in the desert. The old man had discovered the valley while panning for gold deposits more than twenty years prior. Unlike the arid landscape that surrounded it, the valley was lush and green, trimmed with pines and cottonwoods, an oasis nourished by the only reliable water in the Superstition Mountains. He had scooped some of the dirt by the bank of the creek with his bare hand, and, rubbing the grit together between his fingers, he knew at once that the soil could hold seed. It wasn't like the sand and the clay elsewhere in these mountains.

Reavis had wild, pale-blue eyes that were startlingly light. Paired with super-high cheekbones and a full beard, it was hard to look away from the man, but his reputation was built on more than his appearance. He had been married once, but the death of one of his children supposedly drove him mad. He left his wife in California and moved out to the desert, where people said he lived alone. He'd spend most of his time reading, and he'd refuse to enter an establishment where there was a woman present.

He tried his hand at prospecting, supposedly even mining alongside the famous Dutchman Jacob Waltz for a time (read his story on page 166), but he always found himself wandering off into the woods to be alone—which is how he came across the valley.

Almost immediately after discovering it, Reavis, nearly fifty at the time, set new roots. He didn't own the land, but no one seemed to care that he was squatting on it. He built a modest homestead in the middle of the Superstitions, at least a day's journey from the nearest town, where he cultivated and irrigated a plot of some 15 acres. There, he cared for horses, burros, pigs, and chickens, and even grew an apple orchard that spit out fruit juicy enough to trade for clothing, ammunition, and other provisions when he ventured into Globe.

That's what authorities figured he was doing when they found his decomposing body along the footpath out of the valley. It seems obvious that Reavis either ran into someone who wanted his land or maybe a native Apache who wanted him out, but officials said it was a matter of conjecture as to how the sixty-nine-year-old man passed away. In the end, they ruled it "natural causes," as though decapitation had a place among maladies like cancer and heart failure.

DO IT

Make Elisha Reavis's Eden on Earth the centerpiece of a 13-mile out-and-back overnight adventure. From the Rogers Trough trailhead (33.422256, -111.173387), take the Reavis Ranch Trail (#109) roughly 6.5 miles to the ranch, breaking just beneath the saddle around mile 3 to find the faint, unmarked spur to Reavis's grave. Set up your tent in an established site and explore the valley for remnants of the homestead and even the apple orchard, which still fruits. (Eat what you want when you're there, but don't carry any out.) Retrace your steps on the return and watch your head.

Wild Horses

Dead Horse Mesa, East Rim Trail, Dead Horse Point State Park, Utah

THE VISTAS from Dead Horse Point State Park could earn a spot in a scenery hall of fame, if one existed. Located on a sheer-walled mesa that towers above a horseshoe bend in the Colorado River, the park is like an island in the sky with spin-around views of the spires, buttes, and gashes of canyon country. The Colorado, one of the country's largest and most powerful veins, looks almost delicate from this vantage, a teal ribbon that a little girl might tie into her hair.

When the sun sets, consider it a sensory overload. The day's final rays illuminate so many layers in one scene that the rows of sandstone outrun your vision. Everything you think you know about color changes: The reds are redder, the oranges more orange, the golds more golden. And the sky, too: It goes from blue to fire to the softest shade of lavender. Coupled with the far-off whinnying, which is romantic in a way, it becomes a sort of iconic American Southwest experience.

Or, it could be if you don't think too hard about the whole thing.

Because while it's true that perhaps a herd of wild horses is running nearby, it seems likelier that the park's namesakes are returning to the spot where they were murdered.

Sometime in the 1800s, a few cowboys supposedly corralled a herd of wild mustangs on the mesa by fencing off the 30-yard-wide neck where today the park road wends. They selected the best horses—the ones that they could use in their own endeavors and the ones that could fetch them a handsome price on the market—and rode off into the canyonlands. But, perhaps accidentally, they failed to remove the logs and debris they

had used to blockade the mesa, barricading the unchosen horses on the parched plateau.

According to legend, some died of dehydration, but most leapt off the sandstone precipice toward the Colorado River, 2,000 feet below. Hikers today still report hearing the neighing of the ill-fated horses, and, if there's any doubt in your mind, scan down from the overlook at the end of the mesa: There, amid the striations of sandstone in the canyon's wall is an outline of a white mustang.

DO IT

You could drive to the end of the mesa and walk all of 200 feet to get the best viewpoint at this park, but it will taste all the better if you earn it. From the visitor center (38.487626, -109.735780), make a 4-mile-plus circuit that traces the rim of the mesa by linking the East Rim and West Rim Trails (distance varies with how many spurs you tack on). Going clockwise, the Basin, Meander, Shafer Canyon, and Rim Overlooks are each worth the negligible distance off the main loop. Bring an extra memory card for the photo opp at Dead Horse Point, and listen closely.

The Road to Perdition

Horsethief Springs, Ouachita National Recreation Trail, Ouachita National Forest, Oklahoma

WINDING STAIR Mountain is less a peak than a ridge, a lip that stretches more than 32 miles across the Ouachitas. When you stand atop it, in the middle of the Ouachita National Forest, its emerald spine cranes outward in either direction like a gunsight—which is fitting, because chances were good you'd see one of those between your eyes if you passed through here in the 1870s.

Jesse James, the Youngers, and the rest of the outlaws they ran with would hide in the limestone hollows that characterize this area so often that there's a state park named for them not 40 miles away. But they didn't come up to the airy ridge of Winding Stair Mountain to hide; they came here to take what they wanted. They would congregate near a small, freshwater spring on the ridgeline that overlooked the putting-green valleys and pine, oak, and dogwood forests. It was near a relatively high-traffic path, and when unsuspecting travelers passed through en route to Fort Smith or Fort Towson, the bandits attacked.

Mostly, James and company only plundered, but sometimes they killed. Oklahoma was so loosely policed before its statehood, that it generally didn't matter. But "Horsethief Spring" has a better ring to it than "Murder Mountain."

The gang would go on to terrorize more people and wreak havoc in more places before ultimately splintering in 1876 after a failed bank robbery. Their freshwater spring on Winding Stair Mountain remained, strong as ever, however. The Civilian Conservation Corps even built a stone enclosure around it during the 1930s, which you can still visit today. Hikers report feeling an odd sensation of being watched when they do, though.

DO IT

Talimena Scenic Drive passes over the top of Winding Stair Mountain today, but you can't smell the dogwoods from a car. Travel on foot like an old prospector (knowing that laws are better enforced today) on a section of the Ouachita National Recreation Trail midway through a 12.8-mile lollipop-loop. From Cedar Lake (34.778854, -94.692436), take the Horsethief Springs Trail south to the Ouachita National Recreation Trail, which traverses Winding Stair Mountain, before looping back on the former. If you go counterclockwise, you'll pass the springs near mile 6.6. (Turn it into an overnight by camping just below Winding Stair Mountain near mile 7.)

The Wailing Woman

North Rim, Transept Trail,
Grand Canyon National Park, Arizona

N
O GHOST story is comforting, but there's a certain ease of mind when a ghost story has an obvious beginning—when you can trace it back to a specific moment in history. So it's especially unnerving that there is no record, nor any agreed-upon origin, revolving around the apparition of Grand Canyon.

Here's what we know: Hikers have reported seeing a ghost in and near the Big Ditch. Three rangers allegedly saw it on the Transept Trail. When the original Grand Canyon Lodge burned down in the 1930s, onlookers supposedly saw a screaming ghost in the flames. Some employees have claimed that the doors in the rebuilt hotel mysteriously open and close, while visitors have claimed to spot or hear the specter in the area.

There's no rhyme and no reason, just a jumble of seemingly unassociated tales. Except for one crucial detail: In every story, the ghost is a woman—and she's crying. Fittingly, old Mexican folklore tells the legend of a crying ghost. It goes like this: There was a beautiful, young peasant named Maria. Maria's beauty and kindness landed her the attention of a handsome suitor who loved her well and lavished her with gifts. The two married and had two sons before the man began to change. He stopped caring for Maria and his children and would leave them for long periods of time.

One evening, Maria went for a walk along a river to ease her sadness. As she was walking, she saw her husband with another woman who was considerably younger. Driven to uncontrollable rage by her jealousy, Maria drowned her two sons in the river. When Maria came to her senses, she was overcome with grief and self-loathing for what she had done. She

hurled herself into the whitewater and drowned, suffering the same fate as her children.

The legend continues: Maria was challenged at the gates of heaven and not allowed to enter until she had found and rescued her children. Today, she wanders the earth's rivers, weeping, as she searches for her murdered children. She is known as the Wailing Woman, or, in Spanish, *La Llorona*.

The exact whereabouts of the Wailing Woman are hotly debated, but the Grand Canyon features some fifty different rivers, streams, and springs—and a handful of eyewitness accounts of a ghostly wailing woman.

DO IT

There's no shortage of North Rim gems, so don't limit yourself when ghost-hunting. For starters, try the 3-mile, out-and-back Transept Trail from the potentially haunted Grand Canyon Lodge (36.197170, -112.053015), which follows the North Rim (big views) to the North Rim Campground. For a heftier overnight, extra-fit hikers should tackle the Thunder Creek-Deer Creek Loop, a 28-mile behemoth that takes hikers from rim to canyon floor back to rim. To do it, begin at the Bill Hall trailhead (36.434703, -112.430120), then drop into the canyon, cross the Esplanade, parallel Thunder River, descend alongside Tapeats Creek (camp here), parallel the Colorado (prepare for exposure), loop back up alongside Deer Creek (camp here), and reconnect with the Bill Hall Trail; expert navigators only.

The Land of the
Horned Gods

The Great Gallery, Horseshoe Canyon Trail,
Canyonlands National Park, Utah

These are sinister and supernatural figures, gods from the underworld perhaps, who hover in space, or dance, or stand solidly planted on two feet carrying weapons—a club or sword. Most are faceless but some stare back at you with large, hollow, disquieting eyes. Demonic shapes, they might have meant protection and benevolence to their creators and a threat to strangers: Beware, traveler. You are approaching the land of the horned gods.

—Edward Abbey, 1968[17]

H IKERS VENTURE into Horseshoe Canyon hoping—no, knowing—they're going to be watched. It's a rare case, in fact, where that's a good thing, sort of. Because, for all intents and purposes, that's why people go: to stand in a pantheon, face to face with the 7-foot-tall, limbless specters of the Great Gallery.

In the outer reaches of Canyonlands National Park, hidden inside a narrow chasm and tucked beyond gnarled cottonwoods and stunted blackbrush, exist some of the best-preserved rock art panels in the world. Believed to be up to 2,000 years old, the Great Gallery, specifically, has mystified historians, archaeologists, anthropologists, and, yes, hikers over the past century. It stretches 300 feet across the sheer, orange face of

Horseshoe Canyon, displaying more than two dozen broad-shouldered figures with deep-set, hollow eyes—the American Southwest's version of The Last Supper.

Some of the surrealistic figures appear to be wielding sickles and are bent over, perhaps harvesting grain. Some are holding spears, and some stand alongside creatures like mountain goats and, in one case, a dog. It's all beautiful—especially when you consider how long it must have taken the artists to etch each one into the sandstone—until you make eye contact with one of the darker forms. Because while some of the figures appear harmless, or pleasant even, others are holding snakes or marching in formation, their wide, empty eyes staring at passersby. The best that researchers can tell, they're shamans, spiritual intermediaries between this remote corner of Utah and the supernatural.

Take the tallest figure in the Great Gallery at nearly 8 feet: the Holy Ghost, as it's now known. It stands above its seven followers (or "attendants"), with large, tennis ball-size eyes, seemingly melting into the rock on which it was carved. Its creator used a spatter technique to give it an ethereal look—in other words, the artist intended for it to look like a ghost. What that says about the artist is up for debate, but it certainly gives credence to both Ed Abbey's account and those of other hikers that followed.

DO IT

Head over to the Horseshoe Unit of Canyonlands (it's separate from the main park) and find the trailhead off Lower San Rafael Road at 38.473608, -110.200199. From there, follow the Horseshoe Canyon Trail south and into its namesake gash, snaking past visible rock art panels, to the Great Gallery near mile 3.5. The Holy Ghost and His Attendants is on the lower-left side when you're looking at the rock wall—but you didn't need me to tell you that.

Pavla Blanca

White Sands, Backcountry Camping Loop,
White Sands National Monument, New Mexico

HERNANDO DE Luna had a lot to be thankful for—and even more to look forward to. He had seen the fissures of the Grand Canyon and experienced the unmatched depth of solitude of the Sonoran Desert. He likely feasted his eyes on the snow-capped pinnacles of the Sangre de Cristos and dipped his toes in the Rio Grande. And, in due time, he'd begin a life of wealth and opportunity in the New World with the woman he loved.

"When our fathers have built a church in our city to the north," he wrote to his fiancée, "we will be the first to ask their blessing, Manuela. And there we will take our vows."

The young conquistador was midway through a grand expedition to the north, where he'd joined Francisco Vazquez de Coronado in a quest to find the fabled Seven Cities of Cíbola. While the Spanish explorers never did discover the magical lands, they'd met new people and seen new things, and though de Luna couldn't have realized how highly regarded the wilds he traveled through would be regarded today, he still appreciated them. He penned letters to his fiancée, Manuela, often, regaling her with the accounts of his adventures and vivid descriptions of the places he'd seen. His favorite wild place, he told her, was a vast sea of white sand, so out of place and yet so beautiful—not unlike their love.

And it's true: White Sands, at 275 square miles, is the largest gypsum dunefield in the world. The swath of white drifts looks more like a snow-field, stretching on seemingly forever until it abuts the 8,000-foot San Andres Mountains. There is literally no place like it on Earth.

But when the American Southwest failed to meet certain expectations for the conquistadors, legend has it that the company splintered. The relentless Coronado led a band farther northeast into present-day Kansas (read more on page 127), while de Luna and others turned around. There was little point to continuing on a fruitless journey when everything the man loved was back in Mexico City, he thought.

And so de Luna and a small crew began backtracking to Mexico, retracing their steps through the Sangres and heading south. Less than 50 miles from Juárez, however, they ran into trouble. Scaling the toothy Organ Mountains, a chain of crumbly peaks near the border, the men were ambushed by a band of Apache warriors. Presumably, de Luna saw some of his comrades slain and others severely injured, but, perhaps driven by love, he miraculously evaded his attackers and fled from the ridge. Weaving between rocky needles and bounding from precipices, the conquistador sprinted north, landing upon a field of sand so vast and so white, it looked like a blanket of snow.

At some point, back in Mexico City, a young Spanish maiden grew worried, then inconsolable. Resolving to find her groom, she set out for the New World on foot, retracing her lover's steps by clues and details from his letters. Her heart led her to the sea of white sand, where, dressed in a wedding gown, she plodded across the drifts, never to be seen again.

DO IT

Hikers today have reported seeing the ghost of Manuela—an amorphous beauty in a white wedding gown—floating through the dunes after sunset in search of Hernando. Others see her ghost in the sand eddies that sail through the air when the wind whips them just so. See for yourself on the 5-mile Alkali Flat Trail (more of a "route" than a "trail"), the longest established path through the monument. To do it, begin at the parking lot off Loop Drive (32.820469, -106.272908) and hike into the dunes, circling around the bed of Lake Otero. Keep in mind the park closes to day visitors at sunset, so consider gunning for one of the ten campsites. If you nab one, take the 2.2-mile Backcountry Camping Loop from the southern parking lot (32.810091, -106.264593) to pitch your tent in the dunefield. Sunset promises to paint the waves of white spectacular shades of pink and purple—and perhaps bring a visitor of the past.

Pony Up

Palo Duro Canyon, Equestrian Trail, Palo Duro Canyon State Park, Texas

THE RED River War may have been fought over the course of a few months, but it might as well have been won—or lost, depending on your view—on a single day in 1874. It started when the US Army set out to (forcibly) remove the Arapaho, Cheyenne, Comanche, and Kiowa tribes from the Texas frontier, and the Native Americans, predictably, resisted. The two sides skirmished for a few months, but by the late summer, the Indians were running out of resources. And so, led by Lone Wolf, the Native Americans sought refuge in Palo Duro Canyon.

At 120 miles long, Palo Duro is the second-longest canyon in the country, splitting the Texas Panhandle with a geological highlight reel of hoodoos and redrock cliffs. It's technically a desertscape, but it doesn't feel like it: There's reliable water, cottonwoods for shade, spring-perfect wildflowers, and fauna like mule and white-tailed deer, bobcats, coyotes, and wild turkeys. It's a relative oasis for a backpacker, let alone a nineteenth-century refugee.

But on Monday, September 28, 1874, US scouts returned to their base with news: They'd discovered a new trail. They had pinned the Indians. At 4 a.m., the US troops mounted their horses and charged through the paling light to a "wide and yawning chasm," Colonel Ranald S. Mackenzie later wrote. They peered over the redrock precipice and saw more than 200 teepees along the Prairie Dog Fork of the Red River. The troops planned to ambush. But as they slunk into the canyon, a Native American sentry spotted them and set off a mass exodus: It's said that the Indians

ran nearly 4 miles up the rugged gorge to safety. But their refuge didn't fare as well. The US troops set fire to the makeshift village, destroying the Natives' remaining resources. Mackenzie then put the nail in the coffin, so to speak: He ordered his men to capture the Indians' horses. All in all, the US cavalry shepherded 1,448 Arapaho, Cheyenne, Comanche, and Kiowa horses some 20 miles south to the mouth of Tule Canyon. There, they picked out the 400 strongest to add to their own and killed the rest. More than 1,000 horses were shot dead.

With no resources and no horses, the Native Americans were forced out of the Texas Panhandle. The war was over.

But the way it ended didn't sit well with the Natives—or their horses. Shortly after, a few rancheros were camping in the canyon when they heard hooves hurtling down the wash. But when they looked, they saw nothing. Legend says they reported their encounter back in Fort Concho and folks believed them crazy. But more and more folks attested to the phantom herd. Even today, hikers who venture into Palo Duro often report hearing the galloping hooves and whinnying. The Natives may have been removed, but it seems their horses never left.

DO IT

Backpacking is restricted to the park's southeastern corner to protect Comanche and Kiowa archaeological sites (but not horses). To plumb the wildest section, try the 6-mile out-and-back from the Equestrian Camp (34.931811, -101.639078). Follow the Equestrian Trail 1.7 miles, then cut roughly 1.3 miles southeast off-trail to camp on the north side of the fence line (permit required). The park protects the exact location of the rock art, but keep your eyes peeled for etchings of a chief wearing a red war bonnet.

Pacific Northwest

Lady of the Lake

Lake Crescent, Spruce Railroad Trail, Olympic National Park, Washington

MAYBE THEY were intrigued by a dark mass bobbing in the water near Sledgehammer Point. Or maybe it was a small, strikingly white flash at the surface that caught their attention. Or perhaps they simply cast a line for steelhead and were surprised to discover a 5-foot-long bundle on the other end. But on a seemingly random day in July 1940, two trout fishermen reeled in a nearly perfectly preserved corpse. Lake Crescent had surrendered one of her secrets.

Lake Crescent is nestled in a glacially carved valley beneath the Strait of Juan de Fuca on the northern end of the Olympic peninsula. Four-thousand-foot peaks rise on either side, as if guarding it—and maybe they are. The local Klallam and Quileute people tell a story of a once-beautiful region that was marred by war. Mt. Storm King, which soars over the lake's southern banks, grew angry at the tumult and threw a chunk of rock from its peak into the river valley where the tribes were fighting. The boulder killed every one of the battling tribespeople and dammed the water, creating an undisturbed, crescent-shaped lake.

It's more than a legend, though. There's some historical truth to it. Geological surveys indicate that a massive landslide decimated the area 8,000 years ago, effectively separating Lake Crescent and Lake Sutherland. One result of the partition is the former's clear, near-pristine water. Without major inflows, Lake Crescent lacks the usual amounts of plant nutrients, like nitrogen and phosphorus, preventing algae growth.

It's no wonder a floating body looked so out of place in the mirror-like water. The two fishermen, brothers, reeled in the corpse. It was wrapped in

a gray, striped blanket and bound with rope, but tears revealed a shoulder and a foot, both so pallid the body looked less a girl than a mannequin.

"It's like a statue," Sheriff Charles Kemp later concluded after the coroner's examination. "The flesh has turned to some rubber-like substance." There was neither an odor, nor any sign of decomposition. Something about Lake Crescent's unique makeup had not only preserved the body—including a ring of still-purple bruises circling the girl's neck—but had also actuated a chemical process that essentially turned the body into soap. What remained was a woman in her mid-thirties, around 5 feet, 6 inches tall, obviously strangled, and, to an extent, easily identifiable: Hallie Illingworth, missing for three years.

But Illingworth was only one of Lake Crescent's victims. In 1956, an ambulance careened off US 101 at Meldrim Point, plunging into Lake Crescent, killing one. In 2002, a 1927 Chevy was discovered in Lake Crescent's depths, finally closing the case on a couple that had been missing since 1929. They were entombed in Lake Crescent's icy water for seventy-three years. In a chilling interview that was released by the FBI in 2013, convicted serial killer Israel Keyes insinuated that he'd dumped his victims in the cursed lake: "You guys know about Lake Crescent in Washington, right?" he taunted his interrogators.

Who knows how many secrets Lake Crescent hides?

"If you could ever get down (into the underground stream that flows between Lake Crescent and Lake Sutherland)," said Dr. Charles P. Larson, a Tacoma-based pathologist who assisted with the Illingworth examination, "you would probably find from 50 to 100 bodies, all of which have turned to soap."

DO IT

Walk along Lake Crescent's glassy waters—admiring from afar seems safer—on the Spruce Railroad Trail, which traces its northern banks. Find the Spruce Railroad trailhead off Beach Road (48.094863, -123.805016). The path ambles nearly 12 miles south and west along the water to the trailhead on the west end of the lake off Olympic Highway (48.075360, -123.954349). Arrange a shuttle car and do it as a point-to-point, or turn around midway (there is no camping in this area). Keep your eyes peeled for the lady of the lake, a specter that's been seen gliding across the surface and believed to be Hallie Illingworth's haunted spirit.

A Death Trap

Tillamook Lighthouse, Oregon Coast Trail, Ecola State Park, Oregon

"A N ERA has ended," penned the final keeper of the Tillamook Lighthouse. "With this final entry, and not without sentiment, I return thee to the elements. You, one of the most notorious and yet fascinating of the sea-swept sentinels in the world. . . A protector of life and property to all, may old-timers, newcomers, and travelers along the way pause from the shore in memory of your humanitarian role."

Before it was decommissioned in 1957, the Tillamook Lighthouse illuminated the violent Pacific coast for seventy-seven years, guiding ships around the rocky point of Tillamook Head. But had the era truly ended? The light may have been extinguished, but it didn't put a stop to the inexplicable calamities associated with the place.

Located about 1.2 miles offshore in the vicious surf of the Pacific, the Tillamook Lighthouse stands alone on a hunk of rugged limestone. Off the coast of what's now Ecola State Park, it's frequently rainy, more often than not foggy, nearly always windy, and, plainly, brutal. The conditions alone stole the lives of surveyors and construction workers before the lighthouse was even up and running in 1881. But the lighthouse keepers had even more to contend with—isolation, tight quarters, a blaring foghorn, a ghost dog.

Less than three weeks before the Tillamook Lighthouse was lit for the first time, the *Lupatia*, a British barge, lost its course in the heavy fog and wrecked on the rocky outcropping. A dozen of the sailors washed up on the Oregon coast. Four were never found. There was only one survivor: the crew's dog, who swam more than a mile to the shore and relative safety. And yet, the spirit of the dog is said to have remained on the rock at Tillamook Lighthouse, howling for its crew.

Perhaps the ghost dog is responsible for driving one of the lighthouse keepers mad. Holed up in the tiny lighthouse, the man tried to kill another member of his crew by hiding ground glass in his meal. Other keepers reported phantom footsteps and even sensations of things brushing up against them. Many of them pleaded for early dismissals and new posts.

While the era of illuminating the Pacific might have ended in 1957, the hauntings did not. And it didn't help that in 1980 the lighthouse was repurposed into a columbarium. That's right: If you stand on the Oregon Coast Trail, overlooking the lighthouse, you're approximately 1.4 miles away from the cremated remains of thirty humans and the site where at least two dozen more passed. The Tillamook Lighthouse was a protector of life and, now, apparently, death.

DO IT

Skim the western edge of America on the Oregon Coast Trail for the best vantage of the Tillamook Lighthouse. You'll want to knock out the 6.3-mile section that runs through Ecola State Park from the Tillamook Head trailhead at the terminus of Sunset Boulevard (45.973546, -123.954063) to the Ecola Point parking lot (45.919640, -123.974270). If you're going southbound, the spur to the best viewpoint of the lighthouse-cum-columbarium is near mile 3.5 (remember to "pause . . . in memory" here). Retrace your steps or arrange a shuttle car and do it as a point-to-point hike. Overnighting is allowed at Hikers' Camp, near mile 3.4.

A Fool's Errand

Mt. Rainier, Camp Muir Route, Mt. Rainier National Park, Washington

S LUISKIN WAS small, but solidly built. He had a square face that was framed by long, dark hair, though deep creases in his forehead and around his black eyes betrayed his age. But even in the latter half of his life, Sluiskin was made strong by a life lived on the flanks of Takhoma. He owed his life to Takhoma.

The 14,410-foot peak provided the man and his people with food and water, hopes and dreams. But whenever they took the mountain for granted, it reminded them. Sluiskin kept close a story his grandfather had told him of approaching the top of the snow-capped pyramid and nearly succumbing to its fiery demon. Since then, Sluiskin resolved to respect Takhoma's power and steer clear of its blustery summit.

So, when Sluiskin was one day guiding a couple of white men across the snowy slopes of Mt. Rainier and they implored him to take them to the top, he refused. "Don't you go," he begged. "You make my heart sick when you talk of climbing Takhoma. You will perish if you try to climb Takhoma. You will perish and your people will blame me."

Such reverence for the mountain wasn't novel then, and it's hardly novel today, nearly 150 years later. The most prominent peak in the Lower 48, the volcano towers more than 13,000 feet above its base, a cone of ice mantled with evergreens looming 2.5 vertical miles over Seattle. It's so humongous that it generates its own weather, meaning that most of the time, it's buried in its own clouds. But when Takhoma emerges, a mere halo of fog dusting its highest reaches, it's like a religious experience for onlookers.

Seattleites measure their backcountry chops by their adventures on Rainier, which itself belongs on any list of the most challenging peaks in the country. Consider that the behemoth is shellacked with enough glaciers—more than 35 square miles—to effectively swallow Manhattan whole. They cling to its slopes like wads of blue chewing gum, some exceeding 700 feet thick, poised to devour any errant hiker. The shortest route to the summit climbs 9,000 feet, on par with that from Everest Base Camp to the roof of the world. It's no wonder Rainier has become the emblem of the Pacific Northwest, posing on license plates, beer labels, bank checks, and the state quarter.

But despite our deepest respects, the fact remains that Takhoma is one of the country's deadliest peaks. Since such statistics were recorded, Rainier has erased more than 420 lives. Some have been in bulk, like when a 1946 plane smashed into its slopes, killing all thirty-two on board, or like when a 1981 avalanche entombed eleven climbers inside a crevasse. Mostly, though, the mountain picks off people one at a time, usually stealing a handful of lives every year. Some go the way of hypothermia, while others by way of traumatic injuries. Then of course, there are those who have never been recovered, leaving no clues as to how they perished. This all, of course, is nothing, a mere hiccup, relative to how many would surely die if Rainier blew its lid.

Scientists call Rainier an "active volcano at rest between eruptions," which is no more comforting than if they provided an ETA. They suggest that no fewer than 80,000 people would be in grave danger if Rainier blew, spewing ash, lava, and "avalanches of intensely hot rock and volcanic gases" over Seattle.

Perhaps we should heed Sluiskin's warning, after all, though the white men he led in 1870 didn't. The two, General Hazard Stevens and P. B. Van Trump, actually went on to notch the first documented ascent of Rainier, but it wasn't without complications. The men would later describe the harrowing ordeal as utterly miserable, a horrible near-death experience of exhaustion, hypothermia, hunger, and general suffering. In fact, when the two stumbled back to camp, bloodied and beaten, they said Sluiskin eyed them "long and fixedly . . . as if to see whether we were real flesh and blood or disembodied ghosts fresh from the evil demon of Takhoma."[18]

And who could blame him?

DO IT

Normal hikers should consider getting their Rainier fix on any number of the lower trails, which all promise views of the big one with nice bonuses like flora, fauna, and old-growth forests. You can't go wrong. Extraordinarily fit and experienced hikers can tackle the 4.5-mile Camp Muir Route: From the Paradise Visitor Center (46.786474, -121.735481), pick up the Skyline Trail and start climbing. Take it roughly 2.3 miles to Pebble Creek at the toe of the Muir Snowfield. From here, it's about 2.2 miles of glacier travel to Camp Muir at 10,100 feet. This is as high as you can ascend without a climbing permit.

Tunnel Vision

Old Cascade Tunnel, Iron Goat Trail,
Mt. Baker-Snoqualmie National Forest,
Washington

WASHINGTON'S CASCADES are bigger, badder, and denser than anywhere else in the Lower 48. Ranging south from British Columbia, these high-relief mountains create a border of sorts, sealing off the Pacific Northwest from the rest of the country. It's no wonder the Great Northern Railway was considered such an achievement.

In the 1800s, when the West was being settled, engineers had to route the Great Northern Railway up a series of eight switchbacks to surmount what's now known as Stevens Pass (which was, in fact, ultimately named for the railway's chief engineer, John Frank Stevens). It was an engineering triumph that opened the Pacific Northwest to the rest of the world—but it wouldn't last. The Cascades' notorious winter weather routinely shut down the line below 4,061-foot Stevens Pass, burying the rail bed in 25-foot-tall snowdrifts. So in 1900, the Great Northern Railway was rerouted through a 2.6-mile-long tunnel beneath the pass that avoided the switchbacks.

But it was no match for the Cascades. In 1910, a week of relentless snow slammed Stevens Pass, stymieing two trains—one mail, one passenger—at the tunnel's western portal. The blizzard continued to drive into the surrounding peaks, loading 5,386-foot Windy Mountain to the north of the tracks, until its slopes gave way, unleashing the deadliest avalanche in American history. The train cars were swept off the tracks, killing nearly a hundred people.

Although a new tunnel has since replaced the original, the Old Cascade Tunnel remains. Trail builders crafted the old tracks into the Iron Goat Trail, an easy walk—but not for the superstitious. Hikers have reported seeing unexplained shadows in the tunnels' recesses and feeling a heaviness in the air. Some have claimed that they've felt the sensation of hands touching them. Still others have contended that they've heard the phantom *whumpf* of an avalanche, followed by piercing screams and crunching metal. The frequency of strange accounts even inspired paranormal investigators to visit the area.

The ghost hunters promptly compiled a pile of evidence, including audio anomalies and photographs of unexplainable light, to suggest that perhaps the passengers of the ill-fated trains are still trapped in the tunnel—in spirit.

DO IT

We don't recommend entering the Old Cascade Tunnel. Ghosts aside (weird that you wouldn't consider that, but let's say you don't), the tunnel is physically unstable. Your best bet: Drive to the Iron Goat trailhead in Wellington (47.747245, -121.127465) to check out the west portal of the Old Cascade Tunnel. Snap some pictures (watch out for weird light swirls), listen for disembodied screams, pay your respects, then hop back in the car and head 6 miles west on Stevens Pass Highway (US 2) to the Iron Goat trailhead in Leavenworth (47.711299, -121.162237). From there, connect the upper and lower Iron Goat Trails into a 6.6-mile loop that passes a series of interpretive signs as it wends past decrepit tunnels, tracks, and railway artifacts.

History in the Making

The Witch's Castle, Wildwood Trail,
Forest Park, Oregon

D ANFORD BALCH was a rational man who will always be remembered for acting irrationally.

He was a Massachusettsan, a doting husband, and a father who opted to uproot his family in the mid-1800s and head west to make a better life. And so the Balches landed in the Oregon Territory, where Danford had acquired a land claim of some 350 acres amid the forest above the Willamette River. He carved out a plot beneath the sun-kissing Douglas-firs, where colorful buttercups and morning glory are so abundant that today they are considered invasive. No one could blame him then or now.

Legend has it that Danford hired some local help to develop the plot and tend the farm, which is how he came to know one Mortimer Stump. Stump's age is unclear, but he was old enough that his romantic interest in Danford's eldest child, fifteen-year-old Anna, was wildly inappropriate. Danford forbade his employee from courting Anna, but his hardline stance, unsurprisingly, seemed to fuel his teenage daughter's rebelliousness. Within a year, Stump and the young girl fled to Vancouver, Washington, and eloped.

And something in Danford snapped. When the newlyweds returned to Portland in the late 1850s, crossing the slate-colored Willamette in the historic Stark Street Ferry, the inconsolable Danford fired two shotgun barrels into Stump's head. He later claimed it was an accident, and when that excuse gained no purchase, the story goes, he blamed his wife, Mary Jane, alleging that she was a witch who'd hexed him. Neither worked, and the scorned father was thrown behind bars.

But, the enclosure being what you might expect it to be in the unfettered West, Danford escaped. He hid out among the ferns, tiptoeing beneath the Douglas-firs, western hemlocks, and western red cedars of the forest where he'd built his farm, until he was apprehended by the city marshal. In the time that Danford had been evading the law among the towering conifers, Oregon had reached statehood.

In October of 1859, before a crowd of hundreds, Danford Balch became the first man legally hanged in the Beaver State.

After Danford's death, his land passed hands before ultimately ending up in the city's possession. It would be designated Macleay Park, a small piece of the larger Forest Park that dominates Portland. It was further developed for recreational use, and in the 1950s, a century after Danford's hanging, a hut was erected by the Works Project Administration. It's a gothic-looking stone shelter that's being slowly taken over by green mosses and climbing vines. It's creepy in its own right, but positively eerie in that hikers and trail runners who've entered it have reported strange happenings. Some have said they've felt invisible forces brush against them or send chills down their spines. Others have claimed to see amorphous figures floating in the stale air.

It's possible the spirit of Stump has returned to where he met his killer. Or perhaps it's Danford retreating to the setting of the life he had always dreamed of. Or, perhaps Danford was right about Mary Jane all along.

DO IT

Visit Macleay Park beginning at the lower lot (45.535860, -122.712478). Follow Balch Creek on the Lower Macleay Trail roughly 0.9 mile through the corridor of evergreens to where it merges with the Wildwood Trail at the Witch's Castle. Turn around here for a short out-and-back, or continue on the Wildwood Trail for a 5-miler: Climb out of Balch Canyon and cross Cornell Road, ascending to the Pittock Mansion, an opulent estate with a killer view overlooking Portland and, on a clear day, Mt. Hood. From here, retrace your steps to your car.

Stranger Things

Crater Lake, Wizard Island Summit Trail, Crater Lake National Park, Oregon

Two men lost in the forest of the park are never found. . . [Man's] camp and supplies and a 10-foot snow tunnel were located, but not his body. . . The party discovers [a man's] photography equipment, but no trace of [him] is found. . . Four men arrested for stabbing to death another man and dumping his body somewhere on the Rim. . . Skull of [a man] found. . . [Man] disappears while snowshoeing along the Rim. . . Plane wreckage and three skeletal remains are discovered. . .

BODIES MISSING. Drowning victims. Fatal falls. Suicides. Murders. Crater Lake's death record reads more like something you'd expect to find on a seedy crime television show, not the public register of one of our most-coveted national parks. But, there it is: more than a hundred homicides. Throw in the disconcerting frequency with which hikers have reported seeing shadow people, Bigfoot, and UFOs, and the reality is altogether alarming.

It's a startling juxtaposition to the tarn's beauty. More than 7,700 years ago, it's believed that Mt. Mazama, a stratovolcano in the Cascade Range, blew its lid, collapsing and leaving behind a vast crater. Today, that 2,000-foot-deep depression is filled with snowmelt and rainwater, and, since no rivers flow into or out of it, the water remains pure, essentially untouched. The result is a symmetrical pool, the deepest shade of cobalt, framed by evergreens; in its perfect simplicity, Crater Lake looks more like something a child might draw than a real place, which is just as well. The cistern is a hotbed for very strange, inexplicable, *unreal* occurrences.

There's nothing unusual about the atmosphere, and the terrain isn't unusually challenging. But the fact remains that weird stuff happens at Crater Lake. The local Klamaths chalked it up to a feud between gods that left one god's spirit in the blue basin. Paranormal investigators think ghosts are to blame. Rangers have conceded that both are right, and they would know: In addition to homicides, they've filed reports of phantom fires, amorphous figures, and unexplained noises.

And to top it all off, scientific research shows that it's likely Mt. Mazama will eventually blow again, which would surely boost the death toll.

DO IT

Summit Crater Lake's iconic cone on the 3-mile out-and-back to the top of Wizard Island, which rises more than 700 feet above the lake's surface. To do it, park at the north end of Crater Lake (42.981005, -122.083123) and walk about a mile down to the Wizard Island Boat Tour Dock in Cleetwood Cove. Take a ferry across (nationalparkcentralreservations.com), disembarking at the south shore of Wizard Island. From there, switchback roughly 1.5 miles up to the cone's summit, around its top, and back down. The vantage is unmatched, but beware that Klamath legend suggests Wizard Island itself is the head of the spirit that haunts these waters.

West

Gone with the Wind

Bridalveil Fall, Bridalveil Fall Trail, Yosemite National Park, California

YOSEMITE'S DISPLAY of plunging water is the stuff of wanderlust. Three-tiered Yosemite Falls cascades more than 2,400 feet from its upper granite shelf to the valley floor. Sentinel Falls is 2,000 feet tall; Ribbon Fall flows more than 1,600 feet in a near-perfect, well, ribbon of whitewater. Then there's Illilouette, Wapama, Chilnualna, Vernal, Nevada, Bridalveil—and those are just the ones you'll see on a park pamphlet.

They have the power to wow, certainly, but maybe that's because they hold the power to kill. Some 1,000 visitors have died in the park's recorded history, and that number includes an uncomfortably high percentage of hikers plummeting to gruesome deaths in Yosemite's famed waterfalls. In fact, visitors die by way of Yosemite's cascades every year.

Chalk it up to a string of really bad—and regular—bad luck, or consider that perhaps Po-ho-no is to blame. Po-ho-no (literally "Puffing Wind" in the Ahwahneechee language) is an evil spirit thought to haunt Bridalveil Creek, which feeds 620-foot Bridalveil Fall. According to legend, an old woman was gathering grasses at the top of the falls when Po-ho-no lured her toward the cascade's iridescent rainbows and swirling mist. Bewitched, the maiden stumbled forward toward the precipice, closer to the dancing colors, when a gale streamed in from behind her, forcing her over the edge.

Some versions of the legend say that her body was never recovered—because she was imprisoned in the water by Po-ho-no. Today, she, along with Po-ho-no's other victims, entrance others to inch too close to the brinks, blowing them over with spirit-driven winds.

DO IT

You can't hike to the top of Bridalveil Fall—consider that a blessing—but you can visit the basin below it on a short-but-steep, 0.5-mile out-and-back from the Bridalveil Parking Area (37.716747, -119.650912). For a vertigo-inducing view atop a waterfall (read: most dangerous), you'll want to hop on the Yosemite Falls Trail, which climbs 3.4 miles (one way), gaining nearly 3,000 feet, from the Camp 4 trailhead (37.742355, -119.602016). Po-ho-no may haunt Bridalveil, but please use extreme caution on this one. Last option: For a true tour de force of Yosemite's falling water, tackle the 6.3-mile Nevada Fall Loop: From the Happy Isles trailhead (37.732361, -119.559601), link the Mist and John Muir Trails into a clockwise highlight reel, passing photo-worthy views of Illilouette, Vernal, and Nevada Falls.

Into the Wild

The Magic Bus, Stampede Trail, Healy, Alaska

EVERY HIKE is a pilgrimage, but some are more famous. In the States, our Triple Crown long trails are the obvious ones, where dreamers and misfits set out on thousand-mile-long journeys of introspection to conquer whatever demons they may have. It makes sense: No matter where you live, chances are you're close enough to one of the Pacific Crest, Continental Divide, or Appalachian Trails. It doesn't make sense, though, that another one of the most-visited and most-sought-after pilgrimages is some 1,500 miles away from the northwesternmost point in the continental United States.

Tucked in the southcentral region of the Last Frontier in the fringes of the Alaska Range, a seemingly random bus serves as the target for thousands of pilgrims. It's not an ugly corner of the country by any means—bound by 5,000-foot, glaciated peaks to the south—but it is an odd destination choice when the Holy Land of backpacking, Denali National Park, is so close. Further, it's remarkably off the beaten path, or, at least, it was, until September 6, 1992, when a moose hunter discovered the corpse of Chris McCandless in an inconspicuous bus.

McCandless wasn't famous at the time, but quickly became somewhat of a romantic figure in the outdoor space. There's a much better book out there for those interested in reading more about McCandless's life and legacy, but the gist is that he was an idealist and a free spirit who abandoned his middle-class upbringing, donated his $24,000 savings to charity, and embarked on a hitchhiking odyssey across the country. He ultimately landed in Alaska, where the twenty-four-year-old kid resolved to live off the fat of the land. He hitched a ride to the Stampede Trail and, carrying little more than a small knapsack, set out into the bush. He lived in the Magic Bus for more than four months before he passed.

Like a siren call, hikers today try to replicate McCandless's journey, following his footsteps from Healy, Alaska, to the abandoned bus. Some are outdoor enthusiasts looking to notch another life-list trip, some are simply drawn to McCandless's story. But, when they arrive at the bus, they don't often report feeling elated. Instead, they say there's a heaviness in the air, a feeling that perhaps they're intruding in a space where they shouldn't be. Worse, scores of them have become hurt, lost, or stranded by the rising Teklanika River in their pilgrimages. Some have died.

It begs the question: Is a pilgrimage worth it if you never return?

DO IT

It's about 20 miles to the Magic Bus, so plan accordingly. Drive along Stampede Road and park near Eightmile Lake (63.883707, -149.266841). Continue west on the rutted jeep road roughly 10 miles to the Teklanika to set up camp. We do not recommend attempting to negotiate the river if it's higher than knee-level; be prepared to turn around if it is. Remember: This torrent ultimately did McCandless in, sequestering him on the wrong side of civilization. If it's low and gentle, unclip your pack's hipbelt and make your way across. (Need a refresher? Search "cross a river" on backpacker.com.) From there, it's about 10 miles southwest to the bus (63.868240, -149.768672). Leave an entry in the logbook before retracing your steps to your car. Expert navigators only.

The Curse of
Griffith Park

Bee Rock, Old Zoo Trail, Griffith Park, California

DON ANTONIO Féliz may be considered a folk hero in Southern California, but we really don't know much about him—save that he landed upon a 4,000-acre slice of paradise in Los Angeles and later gave it to a Californio by the name of Coronel.

Don Antonio, by a thread of unlikely connections, had himself stumbled into ownership of the sprawling rancho that had once belonged to Corporal José Vicente Féliz, the military escort to the first Spaniards who settled in L.A. By 1860, the bachelor was living on the property with his sister and beloved niece, Petranilla. The latter was blind, but that didn't hinder her appreciation for the natural beauty of the area in which she lived.

At the easternmost tail of the coastal Santa Monica Mountains, the rancho was studded with sandstone outcroppings from which Petranilla could feel the warm Santa Ana winds that drifted through the valley. She could smell the woody oaks and herbaceous coastal scrub or stand in the aquamarine Los Angeles River and let it lick her toes on its course to the Pacific. She may not have been able to see the kaleidoscopic display of blooms every spring, but the birdsong reminded her it was there.

And yet, legend has it that the girl who loved the area most didn't receive it when Don Antonio passed away.

Petranilla was her uncle's only heir—and all but guaranteed ownership of the rancho—but when Don Antonio succumbed to smallpox at the age of fifty-two, his will spelled out a different plan. The beneficiary of the park was to be Antonio Francisco Coronel, the former mayor of L.A. and, until this point, a man curiously absent from Don Antonio's timeline.

Whether Coronel manipulated Don Antonio or not—some versions of the story suggest he fastened a stick to the dying man's head to force him to nod in assent—is a matter of conjecture, but Petranilla didn't care.

"Your falsity shall be your ruin!" she allegedly shouted to the recipient of her home. "The substance of the Féliz family shall be your curse! The lawyer that assisted you in your infamy, and the judge, shall fall beneath the same curse! The one shall die an untimely death, the other in blood and violence! You, Señor, shall know misery in your age and, although you die rich, your substance shall go to vile persons! A blight shall fall upon the face of this terrestrial paradise, the cattle shall no longer fatten but sicken on its pastures, the fields shall no longer respond to the toil of the tiller, the grand oaks shall wither and die! The wrath of heaven and the vengeance of hell shall fall upon this place."

And then Petranilla dropped dead.

Los Angelenos will point out that, shortly after Petranilla's tirade, Coronel's attorney was shot dead, and the probate judge who upheld the transaction soon followed. Coronel's family members grew ill, and, one by one, they succumbed. After Coronel died, each eventual landowner also met an untimely end: One was supposedly shot dead in a saloon scuffle, one was gunned down by an outlaw, and one was pushed by his wife over a banister to his death.

As for the land itself, supposedly the cattle contracted a deadly illness, the dairy business was a bust, wildfires destroyed the grain, and pests ravaged the crops. By the late 1800s, the rancho belonged to Griffith Jenkins Griffith, an aristocrat who allegedly watched a lightning storm wreak havoc on his land—and the ghost of Don Antonio Féliz riding a white stallion among the oaks into the deluge.

After Griffith was nearly shot to death by an employee, he donated most of his land to the city of Los Angeles. It seems obvious why.

DO IT

Hikers today still report seeing a number of ghosts in Griffith Park, including Don Antonio Féliz riding a horse near Bee Rock and Petranilla wearing a white dress near the park headquarters. Visit the former on a 2.4-mile out-and-back from the Merry Go Round lower lot (34.131769, -118.284355). Link the Fern Canyon, Old Zoo, and Bee Rock Trails to the exposed ledge before retracing your steps.

The Underground City

Mt. Shasta, West Face Route,
Mt. Shasta Wilderness, California

Lonely as God, and white as a winter moon, Mt. Shasta starts up sudden and solitary from the heart of the great black forests of Northern California. You would hardly call Mt. Shasta a part of the Sierras; you would say rather that it is the great white tower of some ancient and eternal wall. . . It has no rival! There is not even a snow-crowned subject in sight of its dominion.

           —Joaquin Miller, 1873[19]

SOARING NEARLY 10,000 vertical feet above its base, bursting through a cloak of pines and firs, Mt. Shasta has long captured hearts. Natives deemed it sacred, romantic wanderers like John Muir and Joaquin Miller popularized it, and, today, hikers regard the volcano a rite-of-passage objective. Its devoted return to its glacier-encrusted slopes often—but as chiseled and tanned as the latter may be, young Harvey Spencer Lewis was still surprised to see a lean, 7-foot-tall man emerge from the evergreen forest wearing nothing but a white, satin robe.

The man's neck was draped with strands of gold and rare gems, and his long auburn hair cascaded over his broad shoulders and sinewy back. He had bare feet and padded across the soft earth down Shasta's flank with calculated and deliberate moves. But when he looked up and saw his onlooker, Lewis turned away, afraid to meet the man's piercingly light eyes, for in the middle of the Adonis's forehead was a walnut-size protrusion.

Obsessed with what he claimed to have seen, Lewis, an author, supposedly tracked down other hikers who reported to have seen people of a similar look in the area. He pored over ancient texts and researched history, occult sciences, and Native American lore and could only conclude that the man he'd seen had been of another race not of this Earth. His best guess: The man was part of an underground colony of people that possessed an extra organ—a sixth sense—on their heads and lived in the belly of none other than California's beloved 14,179-footer.

Most, including Lewis, believed the volcano dwellers to be the people of the lost continent Lemuria. Others expanded on the idea, and eventually it was surprisingly widely accepted that somewhere in Shasta's innards was a race of human-like beings who had spent the past 10,000 years building a city of gold festooned with jewels and further developing a sixth sense of perception. Some people reported visiting the city in their dreams and, in some cases, real life.

It seems outlandish, sure, but the theory has persisted nearly a century later. And it's not the only one: Hikers and recreationists have reported seeing Bigfoot, Lizard Man, UFOs, ghosts, and fairies on Shasta's slopes. They've posited that interdimensional portals exist amid the volcano's massifs and that gods transition from the spiritual to the physical through its cone. Put like that, a race of volcano-dwelling beings doesn't seem so outlandish after all.

DO IT

There are some seventeen routes up Shasta. Most climbers—an estimated 90 percent—will take the straightforward Avalanche Gulch, so skirt the crowds and pick something else. Beginner mountaineers should try the 6-mile West Face route from the Bunny Flat trailhead (41.354052, -122.233547), while intermediate mountaineers should try the 5-mile Hotlum-Bolam Ridge route from the North Gate trailhead (41.468311, -122.173809). Find more beta at shastaguides.com, and, as with all mountaineering bids, be prepared to bail if conditions don't suit.

Night Marchers

Nu'uanu Pali, Old Pali Road, Honolulu, Hawaii

A DAY IN the Ko'olau Range has the power to stir any hiker's wanderlust. A fragmented remnant of a shield volcano, the wall of wrinkled cliffs (called "pali" in native Hawaiian) soars a thousand feet out of the Pacific. The folds of emerald escarpments hide horsetail waterfalls, fruit trees, and a menagerie of wildflowers. From their rocky bluffs, top-of-the-world views over white-sand beaches are all but guaranteed.

But darkness tells a different story. In the days leading up to the new moon, ghosts of venerated warriors, chiefs, and even deities comb the area for mortals after nightfall. They parade by torchlight, marching through ancient battlefields to the beating of a drum. Some people believe they're fulfilling their life's work, protecting the highest-ranking chiefs. Others suggest that death has brought them new purpose, as they look to add to their number. People seem to agree, however, that common folks are not worthy to be in their presence. If you make eye contact with a night marcher, you will surely die.

While people have reported encounters with night marchers across the island, there's perhaps no more fitting area for them than Old Pali Road, the site of the state's bloodiest battle.

In 1795, King Kamehameha and his army drove nearly a thousand Oahu warriors over the Ko'olau pali here in their fight to unify the Hawaiian islands. Construction workers who set out to build the original Pali Road—which would connect Honolulu to Oahu's windward side through the southeastern end of the Ko'olau Range—a century later allegedly discovered 800 skulls beneath the cliffs, which became known as the Nu'uanu (literally "leaping mullet") Pali. Some estimates suggest that more than 15,000 warriors were engaged in the Battle of Nu'uanu, so it's not hard to imagine at least some staying behind.

If you sense night marchers approaching—keep an ear out for beating drums or the sound of a conch—strip naked and lie face down. You can't outrun them, so your best bet is to disgrace yourself so badly that they won't want you. Honor their power by dishonoring yourself—that's the idea, anyway.

DO IT

Old Pali Road is an explorable patchwork of trails, old roads, and ruins. For the best introduction, start at the Likeke Falls trailhead (21.372971, -157.791766) and make your way about 1.3 miles south to the Nu'uanu Pali Lookout. Retrace your steps on the return. If the threat of night marchers isn't enough for you, consider researching "Morgan's Corner" beforehand; you'll pass it near the middle of your hike. And, while you should always practice Leave No Trace, it's particularly crucial here: People who've plucked the pretty, viridescent ferns have reported being followed home by dark, shadowy figures—so don't do that.

Urban Legends

Black Star Canyon, Black Star Canyon Trail, Cleveland National Forest, California

THERE'S A campfire story that's told among Orange County hikers. There are, of course, variants, but everyone agrees that it's best told—and listened to—in the craggy canyon in which it takes place.

It begins in the 1830s, when a tribe of Shoshones skirmished with a band of Californians. There's some dispute over the latter, but most people believe that they were rancheros, sort of folk heroes in California history. If that's true, though they were of Spanish descent, then they, too, were natives who, at least in their own opinion, had just as much a right to squat among the pines and madrones of the Santa Anas as the Shoshones. Unimpressed, the Native Americans staged an ambush and stole the Californios' horses.

The white men, it's said, enlisted the aid of William Wolfskill, an acclaimed fur trapper who'd recently led a party of men across the Mojave to settle in Los Angeles. Early portraits depict him with deep-set eyes, a thick brow, and the sort of lipless smirk of a confident man—which he was. He had allegedly fought the notorious Comanches and Apaches and came out on top; he had tracked bear, bison, beaver, and even otter; he had ridden with Kit Carson. By his mid-thirties, when the rancheros sought his help, Wolfskill was already well on his way to becoming one of the wealthiest men in Southern California.

The renowned trapper supposedly led the rancheros to the Shoshone bandits without much effort at all, tracking them up a stream and into the rocky recesses of a crumbly canyon, where the Indians were feasting on horse meat. The scorned rancheros opened fire, massacring the whole tribe in a clearing near their village—present-day Hidden Ranch—in what would later be called the bloodiest battle in the mountains.

This is the story panicked hikers blame when they hear strange noises or disembodied screams in the canyon. It's the tale that paranormal investigators refer to when they see spikes in electromagnetic readings near the supposed massacre site. But, that's not even the half of it.

There's another story of a gruesome murder that took place in Black Star Canyon in 1899. Up until recently, there was an overturned school bus that lay in a ravine spurring its own series of whodunits. The Ku Klux Klan apparently staged meetings between the steep-sided rock walls, while a satanic cult performed rituals, witches met in private, and extraterrestrials touched down. Bigfoot has been spotted here, as well as the ghost of an old miner.

The line between fact and fiction in Black Star Canyon is thinner than the narrow gash itself, so perhaps you should visit and add your own layer to the story.

DO IT

Create a trip up to 11 miles out and back in Black Star Canyon. From the Black Star Canyon trailhead on the road of the same name (33.764337, -117.677922), head north through the gate and along the abandoned road to a junction near mile 0.7. Split east into the canyon and follow it less than 5 miles to Hidden Ranch, the purported site of the bloody battle. En route, you'll pass a waterfall that tumbles more than 50 feet over a rocky precipice and through an abandoned mine shaft. Who knows what else you'll see?

Mine to Lose

Kennecott Mine, Bonanza Mine Trail, Wrangell–St. Elias National Park, Alaska

J ACK SMITH bent down and ran his fingers across the rock. Above, the lofty volcanoes of the Wrangell Mountains were shedding their winter coats, rivulets coursing off the glaciers and streaming across the ground where he stood toward the fireweed-trimmed Nizina River 10 miles away. The rock, wet and washed of any dirt, was undeniably green, "like a sheep pasture in Ireland," Smith later told an investor.

The prospector had unknowingly discovered what would become one of the world's richest copper mines.

The Kennecott Mine—named for the nearby Kennicott Glacier— produced $250,000 worth of copper in its first delivery in 1911. In nearly three decades that followed, prospectors mined more than $200 million worth of ore from its innards. But Kennecott's financial successes hid a very grim truth: The mine, strictly speaking, was a horrible place to work.

"The people in the mine ... [were] all penned up there," one former employee attested. "It was almost like being in prison ... [and makes sense why] there would be 50 or 60 of them that quit [each year]." Another added: "There were miners that got what we called 'miner's consumption' [silicosis] from time to time and [they'd have to go] down to Arizona. Very often they'd have to take a collection for the fare."

The reports are endless: "[The miners] lived without seeing the outside air from the first of November to ... the end of March ... and it was cold. [For $4] a day, [we] worked eight hours and then the company deducted something like $30 a month for board and room.... [We] were essentially captives of the company."

More than half a century later, when a new set of Park Service employees had set out to develop and restore the mine and structures, they, in theory, were treated a lot better. Pay, working conditions, and views, of course, were all improved, but reports began trickling in that the workers would hear strange voices and not be able to identify their sources. Some would claim to see gravesites, and nothing would be there when they investigated. Strangely, more than a few reported that their tools would go missing from their belts, as though someone had nicked them clean.

Even today, hikers to the area say they have experienced similar phenomena in the cradle beneath the hulking Wrangells: disembodied voices, disappearing tombstones, and vanishing gear. Theories abound, but it seems obvious that there is a certain population of the scorned who may be to blame.

DO IT

From the Kennecott Mill Town, begin from the Root Glacier trailhead (61.485615, -142.886853) on the path of the same name. Split onto the Bonanza Mine Trail and take it roughly 4 miles, ascending 3,800 feet, to its namesake. Poke around the old mine (don't enter any structures), or keep going to extend the journey for views of the University Range of the St. Elias Mountains 20 miles east. Do a double-take if you see anything out of the ordinary. Things here aren't always as they appear.

The Crying Boy

Grouse Lake, Chilnualna Falls Trail, Yosemite National Park, California

"**I**WILL HERE relate a personal experience which occurred in September, 1857," wrote Galen Clark in 1904.

Clark, America's first park ranger, would have been forty-three in 1857. He had moved to California's sea of granite peaks a few years earlier to "take [his] chances of dying or growing better" after being diagnosed with tuberculosis. Not only would he survive his bout of consumption, but he would go on to discover the Mariposa Grove of giant sequoias, become a civilian guardian of the area, and ultimately help gain legislative protection for Yosemite. In 1857, Clark was getting things done.

Portraits depict a burly man with a thick, untamed beard and a mustache that covers his mouth. He has high cheekbones and a pronounced brow bone, and he is never smiling. He's often holding a shoulder-height rifle, not unlike the staff of Moses, seemingly daring anyone to try him. Galen Clark was not a man to be trifled with.

It's odd, then, that Clark, a tough, hardy outdoorsman, would make the following admission. In his 1904 book, *Indians of the Yosemite Valley and Vicinity: Their History, Customs and Traditions*, Clark goes on:

> *One day, after a long tramp, I stopped to rest by the side of a small lake about eight miles from the present site of Wawona, and then I named it Grouse Lake on account of the great number of grouse found there. Very soon a party of Indians came along carrying some deer, and stopped on the opposite side of the lake to rest and get some water. Soon after they had started again for their camp I heard a distinct wailing*

cry, somewhat like the cry of a puppy when lost, and I thought the Indians must have left one of their young dogs behind.

Clark explains that he would later join the Miwoks in camp and ask about the yipping puppy.

They replied that it was not a dog—that a long time ago an Indian boy had been drowned in the lake, and that every time any one passed there he always cried after them, and that no one dared to go in the lake, for he would catch them by the legs and pull them down and they would be drowned.

Clark was, of course, spared, but he didn't venture to the water's edge to help the phantom boy. If you hear a wailing child when you visit, perhaps you won't be so lucky.

DO IT

Find the Chilnualna Fall trailhead (37.548377, -119.634190) near the Wawona Visitor Center and take the trail of the same name roughly 9 miles to Grouse Lake (stay hiker's right at both intersections). It's a strenuous route that ultimately gains more than 4,000 feet, so consider applying for a backcountry permit and tenting near Grouse. From there, either retrace your steps to the trailhead, or loop counterclockwise past Crescent, Johnson, Royal Arch, Buena Vista, and Chilnualna Lakes back to the main trail, creating a 28-mile, high-altitude lollipop-loop.

Helter Skelter

Barker Ranch, Goler Canyon, Death Valley National Park, California

I
T BEGAN as a call on a few ruffians who'd been terrorizing Park Service equipment, but Officer James Pursell braced himself for something bigger on October 12, 1969. He and another ranger were investigating an old Chevrolet truck loaded with fifty-five-gallon drums of gasoline that was parked in a rocky wash within the Panamint Range of what was then Death Valley National Monument. Pursell was imposing, with squared shoulders and dark eyes framed by a crew cut, but he and his partner knew they'd need backup.

The officer sat on a small knoll that overlooked the wash and Barker Ranch, a mining cabin that was no longer in use, while waiting for the other rangers. Barker Ranch was small and looked dark, but Pursell and his partner knew that a group of hippies had been squatting in it. And, if Pursell was right, the same transients who were right below his nose were responsible for setting fire to a Park Service vehicle and stealing a few others.

Pursell, fueled by adrenaline, scampered down the small ridge, dodging the cactus spines and white flowers set alight by the brightening moon, to the threshold of the cabin. He had no idea what he'd find on the other side, but clutching a Smith & Wesson .357 Magnum in his hands, the man took a deep breath and kicked the door open.

Before him, a group of long-haired, unclothed miscreants looked up at him, wild-eyed. "Put your hands on your heads!" the officer shouted before ushering them out of the cabin. Pursell grabbed a candle from a nearby table and shone it around the room, looking for stragglers. No one.

He moved toward the bathroom and scanned the small chamber. No one.

But out of the corner of his eye, Pursell saw the tiniest flicker of movement, a swift change in light from the sliver between the cabinet doors beneath the sink.

"If you make one false move, I'll blow your head off!" the officer shouted, pointing his revolver at the vanity.

Slowly, the doors parted. Shaken but not showing it, Pursell angled the candle toward the sink to watch a man uncoil himself from its innards. Long locks of greasy black hair hanging above his shoulders, the man straightened himself and looked up at the officer. A wide, gamey smile slowly spread across his face, a decomposing jack-o'-lantern left on the porch too long.

"Hi," he said, his smirk unbreaking.

Later, in Pursell's pickup truck, the man would tell the officer he had been hiding out in Death Valley to escape an impending racial war that the whites were sure to lose. He asked if he and his girls could be let loose to escape the looming doom. Pursell didn't bite, and the man was taken in and charged with auto theft, arson, and possession of stolen property. In a matter of time, the man would be linked to at least nine murders.

As for Barker Ranch, where Charles Manson and his cult hid out from 1968 into 1969: It remains protected within Death Valley National Park, a strange attraction with a dark history. Some people claim there are more bodies buried in its soil and bloodshed within its walls. Some visitors have reported hearing disembodied chants or seeing the ghost of a man in a white robe. The bravest have hiked to the cabin for the sole purpose of camping inside it, and, not shockingly, have reported feeling haunted in their sleep. Some have described vivid dreams involving Manson himself persuading them to join his cult or commune.

An accidental fire torched Barker Ranch in 2009, which, on some level, seems a good thing—but that doesn't ease the mind much when you see its dilapidated remains, stained black. For what it is, the new look may actually suit it better.

DO IT

The scorched Barker Ranch is off Goler Wash Road in Goler Canyon (35.859631, -117.088594). If you have a high-clearance, four-wheel-drive vehicle, you can technically link a patchwork of Forest Service roads to get there, but a better bet is a cross-country route on foot. From the west side of the park, drive south on Trona Wildrose Road and see how close you can get to Coyote Canyon. If you park at the junction of Wingate and Coyote Canyon Roads (35.858899, -117.179487), it's roughly 9 miles east to the cabin. There are a handful of springs on the route, but call ahead to check if they're running; plan on packing in your water.

Island Time

San Miguel Island, Point Bennett Trail,
Channel Islands National Park, California

JUAN RODRÍGUEZ Cabrillo first laid eyes on the westernmost Channel Island in September of 1542. It rose out of the turquoise Pacific like a beacon, its green slopes smeared with yellow flowers that looked like nuggets of gold against the glittering backdrop of the ocean. Leading a small fleet, the conquistador circled the 500-foot-tall cliffs, where, enclosed between rocky precipices, he discovered a wind-protected harbor. It might as well have been an invitation for the Spaniard.

Cabrillo and his crew had set out from Mexico to sail north along California's uncharted coast three months prior. It was less an exploration than a mission, however, as Cabrillo had supposedly been tasked with finding the mysterious opulent cities that the Spaniards believed existed to the north, as well as a mythical strait that they believed bridged the Atlantic and Pacific Oceans, also somewhere to the north. The expedition had been unsuccessful to this point, and, we know now, would always be, at least relative to its original terms.

But, desperately optimistic, Cabrillo ushered his men onto the windswept isle, where they spent a week or so exploring and recuperating from the past three months' worth of tempests. They encountered some locals, but a language barrier prevented the two from communicating, so Cabrillo and his men moved on.

They touched down as far north as the Sonoma Coast, where the Russian River spews into the Pacific, before storms turned the fleet back toward Mexico in November. But Cabrillo and his men wouldn't make it that far: A raging squall sidelined the crew near present-day Ventura, where they pulled ashore the wind-protected island they'd visited nearly two months prior, declaring it the Isla de Posesión for the Spanish Crown.

But more bad luck beset the crew.

Some accounts suggest that Cabrillo and his men were attacked by natives, but it seems likeliest that the conquistador simply tripped on the jagged rocks of San Miguel's rugged beach. He smashed his shin bone, breaking it clean in half, according to some records. Within a week, Cabrillo's broken leg was gangrenous, and within two, he died, allegedly cursing the island as he succumbed, shouting that whoever tried to claim his island as their own would die a violent death.

To suggest that one conquistador had the power to curse a 14-square-mile mass of land off the coast of California is, of course, ridiculous. But it should be noted that no one lives on the hardscrabble island, numerous ships have wrecked on its rocky promenades, and, fittingly, it was eventually turned into a firing range. After San Miguel was added to Channel Islands National Park in 1980, people weren't even allowed to visit due to the prospect of unexploded bombs. Now they are—the US Navy removed some 125 pounds of munitions and deemed the island safe for hiking in 2016—which is a relief, because how else would we have known that a ghost donning armor and wielding a jeweled sword has been seen roaming San Miguel's wildflower-choked meadows?

DO IT

Buy a round-trip ferry ticket to San Miguel from Ventura (islandpackers.com). At Cuyler Harbor on the island's northeast shore (34.046001, -120.351491), pick up the main trail and take it south to the Point Bennett trail, which meanders west to its namesake, where the seals hang. Out and back, the trip is roughly 16 miles. Back at Cuyler Harbor, visit the monument honoring Juan Rodríguez Cabrillo or set up camp and spend the night (reservation required). Beware the wandering ghost.

Endnotes

1. John G. Whittier, "The Palatine," *Atlantic Monthly* (January 1867): 51–53.

2. Federal Writers Project, *Vermont: A Guide to the Green Mountain State* (Boston: Houghton Mifflin Company, 1937), 360.

3. Samuel G. Goodrich, *The Token: A Christmas and New Year's Present* (Boston: Carter and Hendee, 1830), 257–65.

4. Irvin S. Cobb, "A Witch As Was a Witch," *McClure's* (March 1922): 18–21, 111–16.

5. John Lawson, *History of North Carolina* (Charlotte: Observer Printing House, 1903), 10–11.

6. J. W. Powell, Nineteenth Annual Report of the Bureau of American Ethnology, To the Secretary of the Smithsonian Institution, 1897-98 (Washington: Government Printing Office, 1900), 345–47.

7. Monica P. Wraga, "Waking the Tommyknockers: Mine Said to Be Haunted," *The Gazette* (October 30, 2002).

8. Early Settlers Association of Cuyahoga County, Annals of the Early Settlers Association of Cuyahoga County, Volumes 1-2 (Cleveland: Mount & Carroll, Printers and Stationers, 1880), 366.

9. Melvin Randolph Gilmore, *Prairie Smoke* (Bismarck: Melvin Randolph Gilmore, 1922), 26–27.

10. Mark Twain, *The Adventures of Tom Sawyer* (Hartford: American Publishing Company, 1892), 264.

11. Lansing B. Bloom and Paula A. F. Walter, *The New Mexico Historical Review* (Santa Fe: Museum Press, 1926), 218.

12. Walter Prescott Webb, *The Great Plains* (Lincoln: University of Nebraska Press, 1931), 107.

13. Ella E. Clark, *Indian Legends of the Pacific Northwest* (Berkeley: University of California Press, 1953), 46–48.

14. Truman Everts, "Thirty-Seven Days of Peril," *Scribner's Monthly* (November 1871): Vol. III, No. 1.

15. W. L. Rusho, *The Mystery of Everett Ruess* (Layton, UT: Gibbs Smith, 1982), 98.

16. Edward Abbey, *Desert Solitaire* (Tucson: The University of Arizona Press, 1968), 91.

17. General H. Stevens, "The Ascent of Takhoma," *Atlantic Monthly* (November 1876): 527.

18. Joaquin Miller, *Life Amongst the Modocs: Unwritten History* (London: Richard Bentley and Son, Publishers in Ordinary to her Majesty, 1873), 1.

About the Author

MAREN HORJUS is the destinations editor at *BACKPACKER*, where she produces hiking, travel, and multisport content for the monthly magazine. Her trips section, the Play List, which delivers more than twenty hikes from coast to coast every issue, was a National Magazine Award finalist in 2016. She's been fortunate enough to travel the world in search of prime hiking destinations but remains convinced that the best variety is stateside. She lives in Boulder, Colorado, with her husband and cattle dog.

Acknowledgments

THE FABRIC of this book was first woven inside forts made of bedsheets, when my mom would terrify me and my brother with tales of the nefarious Osh Kosh Mosh. He may have been a product of her imagination, but he still crosses my mind years later when the setting sun casts long shadows across lonely singletrack.

That this book became more than an idea is owed to my *BACKPACKER* family, my wonderful husband, and last, but always first, God.